WOK

CONTENTS

WOK ESSENTIALS

Wok cooking owes its global success to a basic concept which is both simple and compelling: fresh ingredients, fast cooking times, and aromatic spices. Whether it's vegetarian, poultry, meat, fish or seafood, it only takes minutes to rustle up quick, easy and tasty dishes in a wok. This book introduces you to a fascinating kitchen utensil, which has become synonymous with healthy cooking.

COOKING WITH A WOK

Cooking with a wok means more than just dabbling with foreign cookware – it is a journey into the culture of Asia. Woks began to be used in China well over 3,000 years ago. The pot (the meaning of "wok" in Cantonese) was originally developed as a way of preparing a quick meal on one hearth. The invention stood the test of time, with the result that this versatile and extremely economical cooking vessel became widely used all over Asia and now in Europe as well.

We would like to introduce you to this ancient eating culture, which still sees food as a holistic blend of body, mind and soul, and not just as a bare necessity. The principles of Asian cuisine are incredibly simple: when you have finished eating you should feel good. This can only be achieved if the food is well-balanced, which means that the ingredients have to meet the following basic requirements:

- fresh seasonal produce
- fast cooking times
- aromatic spices

Asian kitchen utensils have been perfected to the same degree as the art of cooking. Let's start with the wok, the big pan with the rounded base. With its classic design and robust construction, it is also very energy-efficient – a key factor in ancient China when firewood was scarce.

Since Asian cooking has become popular, woks have been available in different shapes, sizes and materials. If you feel like investing in a wok, see how it feels in the shop when you hold it. Woks come in two styles: with two loop handles or a single stick handle. Both versions are equally user-friendly.

Besides the wok itself, you can also buy accessories designed to make it easier to cook and prepare Asian dishes. Most woks are sold as part of a set. Anything else you need can be found in specialist Asian shops and now more widely on the high street as well.

Metal rack
Every wok should have a metal rack, which is usually semi-circular. It is attached to the rim of the wok for draining deep-fried food once it is cooked and to keep it hot.

Lid
A lid is a basic accessory of the wok. Used mainly for steaming, it is generally made of stainless steel, aluminium or heat-resistant glass.

Spatula
The spatula looks like a small shovel with a raised edge. The bottom edge of the metal plate is slightly rounded to prevent food from being damaged when stirring and lifting. The handle of the spatula is fairly long, made of wood or plastic.

Skimmer and bamboo sieve
There are two different types of sieve: a skimmer with fine to coarse mesh and bamboo or wooden handle, which is used to lift the fried food out of the oil or to move it around to ensure even browning. You also get bamboo sieves in various sizes, with or without a drip tray, or smaller mesh sieves with a stick or bamboo handle.

Cooking chopsticks
Real pros use cooking chopsticks to stir food around in the wok. They are longer than the chopsticks you eat with, so that you can reach the bottom of the wok without burning your fingers.

Bamboo tongs
Bamboo tongs are for taking small pieces out of the wok for testing or to lift cooked food out easily. Tongs are especially useful for anyone who finds it difficult to handle chopsticks.

Wok whisk

Whisks are another useful and traditional wok accessory with multiple functions. They are used to stir-fry very finely chopped ingredients, as the fine ends of the whisk are better suited to this than a large spatula. The whisk is also useful for cleaning the wok under hot running water. Made from thin bamboo strips, whisks should never be cleaned with detergent: rinse well after use and air-dry.

Steamers

Steaming is the most common way of cooking vegetables and fish in China. Bamboo steamers, which come in various sizes, are covered with a lid then placed on a rack in a wok filled with boiling water (to just below the bottom of the steamer). The rising steam permeates the little basket without the food coming into contact with the water. Because the steamers are not only functional but attractive as well, they are also a popular way of serving food.

Kitchen cleaver

If you are not daunted by an authentic approach to the task in hand, equip yourself with an Asian-style food cleaver and associated chopping board. There are many uses for this type of cleaver in Asian cooking. As well as for fine and coarse chopping, it can be used to fillet, pound and beat meat. Asian cooks usually have three types of cleaver in different weights for different purposes.

Chopping board

Round hardwood sections, cut in a single piece from a tree trunk, are highly prized items in Asian kitchens. The best options on sale here are laminated/ bamboo boards, or blocks.

PREPARATION AND COOKING

Great importance is attached to preserving the colour, structure, smell and taste of dishes in Asian cooking. So the individual ingredients must be combined in a balanced, harmonious way. These elaborate preparations take considerably more time than the cooking itself. By finely chopping ingredients the cooking time can be kept to a minimum.

It also makes sense to cut the quickest-cooked ingredients into larger pieces than the ones which need longer to cook.

Ingredients with different cooking times can also be blanched or pre-cooked so that everything cooks together evenly. Various herbs and spices should be gently roasted to flavour the oil for the next ingredients.

COOKING TECHNIQUES

Stir-frying

Stir-frying is the most popular and widely used method of wok cooking. The ingredients are heated up in a very small quantity of very hot oil, and are continuously moved around the pan at the same time. This means they are cooked in minutes, without losing any natural flavour, vitamins and nutrients. Meat becomes nice and crispy on the outside, while retaining its juices. Vegetables stay crunchy and firm to the bite. As stir-frying is an incredibly fast process, it is crucial to have all the ingredients prepared in advance.

Braising

Braising involves firstly frying or searing fairly small amounts of ingredients in the wok; liquid (water, seasoned stock, etc.) is then added, and it is left to simmer gently, covered with a lid. This method is especially good when cooking coarse-fibred meat. Red-braising is a classic style of Chinese cooking, which gets its name from the large quantity of dark liquid, such as soy sauce, in which the dish simmers after being sautéed.

Deep-frying

In deep-frying the ingredients (raw or dipped in batter) are cooked in hot oil. Deep-frying in a wok uses far less oil than traditional methods. Make sure the oil is at the correct temperature, i.e. hot enough. To check this, dip a wooden chopstick into the oil. If little bubbles rise up, you can start deep-frying.

Steaming

Steaming is the most traditional cooking method used in China. The ingredients are placed in a soaked steamer, which is in turn put in a wok with a small amount of water, and the food is then cooked in the steam. When steaming, it is important that the steamer and food do not come into contact with the liquid in the wok; the wok must also be tightly closed with a lid.

Boiling

Woks are regarded as good all-rounders, and with good reason. So naturally you can use them for boiling as well. Soups and stews can be made in a wok, by firstly sautéing the ingredients, then adding liquid and leaving it to simmer. Preparing meat in a wok – boiling it first and then frying it – is a time-consuming but delicious process. The end product is meat that is incredibly tender on the inside, while crispy on the outside.

Baking

The eminently versatile wok can also be used for baking. The classic wok is hemispherical in shape, with a curved bottom. In European versions, however, the bottom of the wok is usually flat so that it is easier to use on traditional electric cookers. Small pancakes can be made in a wok, as well as spring roll pastry or little stuffed dumplings with a spicy filling (like rotis) which are fried in hot oil.

COOKING VEGETABLES IN A WOK

Vegetables and woks are a match made in heaven. Vegetables can be cooked in minutes without losing their natural flavours, vitamins and nutrients. As they remain crunchy and full of flavour, the basic requirement of freshness and simplicity in Asian cooking is met.

Asian cuisine has some exotic vegetables which make wok-cooked vegetable dishes even more appealing. There are white aubergines from Thailand, and pak choi from China – a mild mustardy-flavoured cabbage similar to Chinese leaves. Okra is the long, unripe fruit of a plant from the mallow family, and water chestnuts are the dark-brown, bulbous fruits of an aquatic plant (with nothing in common with nuts, other than the fact you have to shell them). On the other hand bitter cucumber and yardlong beans are similar to common counterparts here. Yardlong beans, which are about 30 cm in length, are great for cooking in a wok. If unavailable, they can be replaced by runner beans. Another exotic ingredient is lotus root, which you can buy fresh or pickled.

Another essential wok ingredient is all the different Asian mushrooms, such as oyster, straw, shiitake, mu-err or nameko varieties. Straw mushrooms are cultivated Chinese mushrooms with a delicate flavour. They have a greyish-black, dome-shaped cap and cream gills. By contrast, shiitake mushrooms are very aromatic tree mushrooms, used to flavour many dishes and credited with medicinal properties in Asian countries. As mu-err mushrooms look like ears, they are also called cloud-ear mushrooms. Nameko mushrooms are Japanese sheathed woodtuft. Not all mushroom varieties are always available fresh, but they can be obtained in dried form.

Vegetables can be cut into pieces, slices or strips according to taste. Very hard vegetables like carrots, cucumbers, celery or radish can be cut into even slices using a mandolin, or a potato peeler for very thin slices. Leafy vegetables should be chopped into wider strips of about 3 cm as they wilt rapidly. There are no limits to your imagination. Cutting the vegetables diagonally into slices or strips gives a very decorative effect.

RICE – GIFT OF THE GODS

In Asian cultures, eating rice is pretty much synonymous with eating, full stop. A meal without rice is unthinkable. There must be something really special about this ancient cultivated crop for almost half the world's population to have adopted it as its staple food. Rice is the perfect accompaniment to well-seasoned Asian meat, fish and vegetable dishes. In the flowery language of the Orient, the saying goes that "... rice ushers the other food pleasantly into the stomach...".

We too have been paying more attention to rice in recent years. For we have now realised just how many vital substances are contained within the little grains: vitamins, minerals, carbohydrates, trace elements, fibre, and lots of high-grade protein that is easily digested. Added to

which, it can be prepared fairly quickly and in a variety of ways, as well as being filling but not too heavy on the stomach. There are around 8,000 different types of rice which are divided into three categories according to their shape: long grain – medium grain – short grain.

As the name suggests, long-grain rice is long, thin and quite hard. When cooked it becomes nice and fluffy and keeps its shape. The best-known variety is Patna rice, which is also available commercially as brown and parboiled rice. A special process allows parboiled rice to preserve nutrients that are usually lost during other refining processes like whitening and polishing. A special Asian delicacy is basmati or fragrant rice, which makes your mouth water at the very thought! As well as their rounded appearance, medium- and short-grain rice are also softer on the inside than the long-grain variety. Wherever chopsticks are used in Asia, people prefer white, short-grain rice. The obvious reason for this lies in the use of chopsticks. While the grains remain dry and separate when cooked, they stick together slightly, so they are easier to eat with chopsticks. At any rate, cooking rice is by no means as hard as it seems. Our failsafe method is to cook it Chinese-style, as follows: Put two cups of dry rice into a pan. Add three cups of water and salt to taste. Bring it to the boil, cover with a lid, and turn it down immediately to simmer until all the water has been absorbed by the rice.

This gives you five cups of cooked rice.

Rice is not only the staple diet in Japan, it is food and culture rolled into one. The little grains were once so valuable that having "white gold" was a measure of overall wealth. Even Samurai warriors were paid in freshly harvested rice. To this day people who have been forced to move from the land into cities still have a sack of freshly picked rice sent to them from their home villages. Young rice tastes so intensely of earth, air, sun and

water that it should never be spoiled by ingredients that detract from this wonderful taste. The philosophy behind Japanese cooking is difficult for Europeans to grasp, however, as we tend to regard rice as a filler, albeit a tasty one, which is necessary to varying degrees.

NOODLES – HAPPINESS IN A BOWL

Noodles contain the promise of a long and happy life, according to an old Chinese proverb well-known throughout Asia. So it is hardly surprising to find so many different types of noodles forming the basis of a whole range of dishes, as well as being a feast for the eyes. In Asian cuisine, noodles compete with rice in the popularity stakes, and are even the staple diet in some regions. Even there, however, noodles were unable to squeeze rice out completely, as they are partly made with rice flour.

Glass noodles, for instance, are made from mung bean starch, and stay transparent even after soaking. After pouring hot water over them, leave them to soak until they have swollen up: there is no specific cooking time. In the meantime you can cook all the other ingredients and then stir in the well-drained noodles. As these noodles have a neutral flavour, they combine perfectly with all spices.

Rice noodles are dried, almost transparent, and turn snowy-white after soaking, unlike glass noodles. As the name suggests, these noodles made from rice flour have the same delicate flavour as rice. Rice noodles come in different widths, from very thin to broad ribbons. Deep-frying them briefly from their dried state produces a very decorative effect.

The egg noodles most similar to the ones found in Europe are very popular in Thai cooking. The only difference is that, in Thailand, goose or duck eggs are used to make them instead of hen's eggs. What are basically standard ingredients are also given a distinctive aroma through the addition of a hint of dried shrimp or seaweed.

A huge selection of both egg and wheat noodles, in all sizes and widths, is available in Asian shops. Noodles are usually pre-cooked so that you only need to soak them or pour boiling water over them. In some well-stocked Asian grocers you occasionally find fresh ones on sale. If you get the chance, don't on any account miss this unique culinary experience.

COOKING MEAT AND POULTRY IN A WOK

The special way of cooking meat and poultry in a wok turns them nicely brown and crispy on the outside, while the inside remains tender and succulent. There is no healthier and faster way of cooking meat and poultry than by using a small amount of oil and extreme heat. As wok cooking is such a fast process, meat and poultry must be prepared in advance. Beef and pork are best cut into thin strips and lamb into cubes. Chicken and duck should be sliced into goujons.

Normally the first step is to sear the meat briefly in a small amount of very hot vegetable oil: the different types of meat will take longer or shorter times to cook. Lean chicken takes less time to cook than beef or pork. The meat should be turned and stirred continuously when browning. After a couple of minutes the meat will be ready and can be lifted out of the wok and put to one side. The vegetables and other ingredients can then be browned in turn as well. Finally the meat is returned to the wok, and then all the ingredients are mixed thoroughly and quickly heated up again.

An even better flavour can be obtained by marinating the meat before cooking. This involves leaving the finely chopped meat to soak in classic Asian sauces which have been pre-seasoned with herbs and spices. Marinating makes beef in particular tenderer and tastier. Each type of meat partners up best with specific spices, herbs and vegetables. Chicken's mild flavour is best suited to sweetish aromas, while duck should be strongly seasoned. Pork can be used in versatile combinations, in either elegantly simple or sophisticated recipes. Lamb, with a distinctive taste all of its own, also combines well with both exotic flavours and bland vegetables.

FISH AND SEAFOOD

Countries in Asia are surrounded by sea, so fish and seafood have traditionally played a key role in Asian cuisine. All seafood and river fish, as well as mussels, prawns, lobster, crabs and especially squid, are suitable for wok cooking. Fish should be cut into bite-size pieces before cooking, though it can also be cooked whole.

If fish dishes contain vegetables, start by cooking the vegetables, as most of them require a longer cooking time than fish. This prevents the fish from falling apart.

In principle fish and seafood partner well with both hot spices and sweet and sour flavours, as well as vegetables or exotic fruits like pineapple or mango.

For squid, which can sometimes be a bit tough, here is a tip to make it tender. Cut open the squid tubes, and lay them on the work surface with the inside facing down. Using a sharp knife, carve out diamond shapes on the outside. The squid pieces then curl up during cooking, giving a very decorative effect.

Prawns, also called shrimps or king prawns, are found in many varieties in all of the world's oceans. Tiger or king prawns, which are native to the subtropical waters of the Indian and Pacific Oceans, are mainly used in Asian cooking. Prawns should be shelled from the underside. Then, using a knife, make a cut along the back to remove the black vein.

If you marinate the fish pieces before cooking they are really delicious. Classic Asian sauces can be used as a marinade – fish, oyster, soy, hoisin, or

even rice wine. The marinade gets its distinctive aromatic quality from the exotic herbs and spices, like lemon grass, chillies, ginger, or even honey, which constitute the special charm of Asian cooking.

Scallops have a lovely tender flesh. Ideally you should buy them in shells and open them yourself. Hold the scallop

firmly with the flat side up, carefully run a knife between the shells and prise open the scallop. Remove and discard the greyish flesh inside the shell, leaving the white muscle meat and red coral (or roe) free to use in cooking.

Mussels are subject to strict quality control and must be absolutely fresh. When you buy them and before you

begin to cook, you should ensure the shells are tightly closed, or that they close immediately when tapped. Any open ones must be picked out. Mussels open up during cooking; if they don't, make absolutely sure you discard any mussels that remain closed.

A TO Z OF INGREDIENTS

Alfalfa sprouts
come from a forage crop also known as lucerne. (Fig. 1)

Allspice
The seeds of the pimento tree, which taste like a cross between cloves and peppercorns, are called allspice. They should be used either whole or freshly ground. Also known here as Jamaica pepper, allspice is refined and used with bay leaves in fish or meat broth. (Fig. 8)

Bamboo shoots
are the young, edible shoots of a specific type of bamboo. They have a delicate, nutty flavour and are very popular as a hot or cold vegetable in Asian cooking.

Bean curd
better known here as tofu, is a high-quality vegetable product made from cooked soya beans. Tofu is rich in easily digested protein (approx. 10–13 g per 100g), vitamins and minerals, but has virtually no cholesterol. It is an extremely versatile ingredient. Since the boom in Asian cuisine, tofu is

also available in a range of flavours in the West – from natural (unflavoured) to strongly spiced, smoked or marinated.

Bonito flakes or powder
are made from dried salt-water fish, mainly tuna.

Cardamom
tastes a bit like cinnamon and cloves. The seeds of this reed-like plant are used as seasoning, and they too have both medicinal properties and a distinctive flavour. (Fig. 5)

Chillies
Chillies are the fruit of the *Capsicum* pepper plant. Their colour (green, yellow or red) gives an indication of how mild or hot they are; and the smaller, the fierier. The seeds are mainly responsible for the piquancy: if you remove them before cooking they will be a bit milder. (Fig. 3)

Chopsticks
are the "eating tools" in many Asian countries. Only in countries where the Chinese influence is less pronounced, like Thailand, Indonesia, Malaysia and the Philippines, do they mainly eat with a spoon, occasionally with spoon and fork, or simply using their fingers. That said, there is more than one kind of chopstick. Irrespective of the size and appearance, however, they all serve the same purpose: the user concentrates on the food, eats slowly, enjoys the food and digests it well.

Coconut milk
is not the liquid inside the nut, but is instead obtained from the fruit's flesh. You can make it yourself by finely grating the white flesh and blanching it in the same amount of hot water. Leave it to soak and then press it through a muslin cloth. You can also use dried flakes or unsweetened, tinned coconut milk.

Coriander

Also known as "Chinese parsley", coriander shares only the appearance of this herb, not the flavour. The whole plant is used in Asian cooking: the aromatic leaves, pepper-sized seeds (whole or ground, which taste like cinnamon and nutmeg), and the roots. This annual plant is easily grown in every vegetable garden. (Fig. 6)

Cumin

looks a bit like our native caraway seeds, and has similarly beneficial effects for the digestion. The taste is quite different, however, so caraway cannot be used as a substitute for cumin. If you want to know what cumin tastes like, try some bitters, as this is where it is mainly used in Europe.

Curry

is a spice mixture blended according to taste and usage in every Asian household. The important thing is to make sure the five flavour types – sweet, sour, savoury, mild and hot – complement each other. If you want to make an authentic mix, dry-roast the dried spices (e.g. cardamom, cumin, turmeric, pepper, cinnamon, cloves, chilli and mace) briefly in a pan without oil (be careful, as they burn easily), allow them to cool, and then grind them using a mortar and pestle. The mixture can be stored in well-sealed glass jars in a cool, dark place for some time.

Curry pastes

are the basis of many Thai dishes, giving them their typical flavour. Made up of a wide variety of spices and herbs, they can be either mild or hot depending on the ingredients. Their full aroma is released by grinding them with a mortar and pestle.

Five-spice powder

Each country has its own blend, based on fennel seeds, cloves, cardamom or pepper, star anise and cinnamon.

Galangal

A member of the ginger family, galangal should be peeled before use, and then cut into thin slices or finely chopped. Galangal tastes a bit like ginger, but is not quite as hot.

Ginger

is the soul spice at the heart of Asian culture. The great

3

4

Confucius always used ginger at mealtimes, a personal recommendation of the highest order. The yellowish-brown, gnarled roots contain active antibacterial substances which are also good for the digestion. If possible, ginger should be used in its fresh form, as this releases its spicy-hot flavour to the full.

Hoisin sauce
is the best-known sauce, along with soy sauce, in Asian and especially Chinese cooking. It is produced from soya beans according to a traditional recipe, and comes in different flavours.

Kaffir lime
For a citrus flavour, Thai cuisine uses the peel and leaves of the kaffir lime. The peel is finely chopped and added to dishes, while the leaves are either cooked whole and removed before serving, or finely chopped into the dish and consumed. (Fig. 4)

Lemon grass
is a perennial scented grass with a delicate citrus flavour, which is partly lost when dried. It is occasionally found in its fresh form in delicatessens here, or dried whole. More recently it has been available ground as well. If you are unable to find it, use finely zested lemon peel.

Mangetouts
are very small bright green pods with sweet-tasting peas. They are easy to grow in a vegetable garden, but must be picked at just the right time. If they are left too long, they lose their sweetness and can no longer be eaten whole.

Mirin
is a slightly sweetened rice wine. A good substitute is dry sherry.

Miso
is a fermented paste made from rice, soya sprouts or barley, and soya beans. It comes in many varieties.

Mu-err mushrooms
are also called "cloud-ear mushrooms" on account of their appearance. They are usually dried, so they must be soaked in water before use.

Nam Prik
is a Thai dipping sauce, much like Indonesian sambal. Its main ingredients are chilli,

5

6

garlic, shallots and shrimp or prawn paste.

Nutmeg and mace

are spices from the same tree. The size of a walnut, the nut is covered by the aril, or mace. When freshly grated, nutmeg releases its bitter flavour. Mace can be used whole in cooking or broken into pieces, but should be removed before serving. (Fig. 7)

Oyster sauce

is a thick brown condiment. It is rather salty and should be used sparingly. (Fig. 2)

Palm sugar

is used to season both sweet and savoury dishes. Palm sugar is sold in solid blocks, but you can replace it with brown sugar if need be.

Rau om

is a perennial plant with aromatic, sweetish leaves that taste like cumin. Rau om is very widely used in Thai and Vietnamese cooking.

Saffron

is obtained from the stigmas of a variety of crocus, and is a very expensive spice.

Sambal oelek

is a red-hot, fiery paste made from chillies, which should be used sparingly. (Fig. 9)

Sesame oil

is a very aromatic essence used for frying (light oil from unroasted grains) and as seasoning (dark oil from roasted grains).

Shiitake mushrooms

are Japanese cultivated mushrooms. As well as being full of flavour, they generate little waste, are suitable for freezing and drying, and more importantly, they do not contain any pollutants.

Soy sauce

This indispensable sauce in Asian cooking comes in a wide range of flavours and two types – light and dark. The light version has a mild taste and will add flavour to the food. The dark sauce is stronger, thicker and adds extra saltiness to dishes.

Spring onions

are milder than their common siblings, large and small. The "spring" part refers to their green, delicate appearance rather than when they are harvested. In fact these delicate little onions are

7

8

available practically all year round.

Star anise
looks like a star and tastes of aniseed. It can also be replaced by aniseed or fennel seeds.

Tamarind
is a tart, pod-shaped fruit used to make sauce, paste or purée. The name means "Indian date" in Arabic. (Fig. 10)

Tempura flour
is an extra-fine flour which is used to make the classic batter.

Thai basil
has very little in common with European basil. Its leaves are firmer and it has a slightly aniseed taste. (Fig. 11)

29

Thai chives

We cannot imagine Thai cuisine without these chives, also known as Chinese chives. They smell like chives and taste of garlic. (Fig. 12)

Tofu

See *Bean curd*

Turmeric

gives curry its classic yellow colour and has a mild peppery, slightly bitter taste.

Water chestnuts

are the dark-brown, knobbly fruits of an aquatic plant. Also known as Chinese water chestnuts, they are only available here in cans. They can be replaced by bamboo shoots.

Wonton wrappers

are thin sheets of dough made from rice flour.

11

12

SOUPS

In Asia soups represent a bustling marketplace of Far Eastern delicacies. Even in the simplest clear soup, different tastes are subtly blended together in a perfect match, following age-old traditions.

FISH SOUP WITH TOFU

SERVES 4

600 g plaice fillet
1 cucumber
3–4 tbsps sesame oil
1 finely chopped onion
1 finely chopped garlic clove
½ tsp each of ground star anise and ground cinnamon
1 litre fish stock (fresh or a cube)
2–3 tbsps soy sauce
2 cl aniseed-based spirit (e.g. raki, arak, pastis)
200 g tofu

PREPARATION TIME:
approx. 35 minutes
306 kcal/1285 kJ

1 Wash, dry and chop the fish fillets into small pieces. Peel the cucumber, halve it lengthways, and remove the seeds. Cut the cucumber into wedges.

2 Heat the oil in the wok and fry the fish and cucumber pieces for 2–3 minutes. Add the finely chopped onion and garlic, star anise and cinnamon.

3 Pour in the stock or crumble the fish cube into the soup. Stir until dissolved. Season the soup with the soy sauce and aniseed schnapps. Cook on a gentle heat for about 10 minutes. Cut the tofu into small pieces and add to the soup 3 minutes before the end of the cooking time. Ladle the soup into small bowls and serve.

DID YOU KNOW?

Plaice can be up to 3 feet long, but the ones found in shops are usually about half this size. The youngest, smallest plaice caught in spring have the most delicate flavour and texture.

SORREL SOUP

1 Wash, pat dry and roughly chop the sorrel. Finely chop the dates. Rinse the hearts of palm and cut into small pieces.

2 Heat the oil in the wok and briefly sauté the hearts of palm and dates.

3 Pour in the vegetable stock and season with salt, pepper, ground ginger and ground cloves.

4 Add the bean paste and simmer for about 10 minutes. Pour in the coconut milk and cook for another 1 or 2 minutes, stirring continuously.

5 Dry-roast the sesame seeds in a pan. Divide the soup into small bowls and serve sprinkled with sesame seeds.

SERVES 4

400 g sorrel

5 dried dates

100 g hearts of palm (tinned)

3–4 tbsps groundnut oil

500 ml vegetable stock

Salt and pepper

Ground ginger and ground cloves

2–3 tbsps spicy black bean paste

250 ml unsweetened coconut milk

2–3 tbsps sesame seeds

PREPARATION TIME:
approx. 20 minutes
264 kcal/1110 kJ

35

ASPARAGUS AND PRAWN SOUP

1 Bring the chicken stock to the boil. In the meantime wash the asparagus and cut them in half. Cook the asparagus in the boiling stock for about 5 minutes, then lift out and set aside.

2 Remove the vein from the prawns, wash and dry them. Peel and finely chop the shallots.

3 Heat the oil in a wok, then sweat the shallots in it for 2 minutes. Add the asparagus, prawns and stock. Boil for 3 minutes.

4 Remove the wok from the stove. Mix a little water into the cornflour to make a paste, then add it gradually to the soup, stirring well.

5 Heat up the soup again until it thickens slightly. Stir in the fish sauce, salt and pepper.

6 Beat the egg and add it to the soup, stirring vigorously to produce threads. Serve sprinkled with chives.

SERVES 4

1 litre chicken stock
300 g green asparagus tips
200 g shrimps or prawns
4 shallots
1 tbsp oil
1 tbsp cornflour
2 tbsps fish sauce
Salt
Pepper
1 egg
Some chives for garnish

PREPARATION TIME:
approx. 20 minutes
(plus cooking time)
100 kcal/418 kJ

SPICY DUCK SOUP

SERVES 4

400 g duck legs, or left-over roast duck

1–2 tbsps groundnut oil

3 red chilli peppers

3 garlic cloves

3 shallots

3 tbsps fish sauce

100 g oyster mushrooms

2–3 tbsps chilli sauce

500 ml coconut milk

500 ml duck stock (available online, use good chicken stock, or make your own)

A handful of Thai basil

PREPARATION TIME:

approx. 25 minutes

553 kcal/2325 kJ

1 Remove the skin and bones from the duck and chop the meat into small pieces. Heat the oil in the wok and sear the duck meat in batches. Remove from the wok and keep them warm.

2 Cut the chillies in half, de-seed them, wash under cold running water, and cut into strips. Peel and slice the garlic cloves and shallots.

3 Mix the chillies, garlic and shallots with the fish sauce and stir-fry in the oil used to fry the duck for 3–4 minutes.

4 Trim, wipe and finely chop the oyster mushrooms and add to the wok. Pour in the chilli sauce, coconut milk and duck stock, then add the duck meat. Cook gently for about 6–7 mins. Wash and pat dry the basil, then cut into fine strips. Add to the wok and cook for about 2 minutes. Ladle the soup into bowls and serve.

 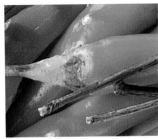 

RICE NOODLES WITH CRAYFISH

1 Soak the noodles in plenty of warm water until soft. Drain well in a sieve, and rinse with cold water.

2 Heat up the lobster stock in the wok, along with the ginger juice, soy sauce and lemon pepper. Gently cook the noodles in the liquid for 3–5 minutes.

3 Add the crayfish and heat up. Whisk the eggs and slowly pour them into the rice noodle mixture. Allow it to thicken for a minute on a low heat, then gently stir. Ladle the soup into small bowls and serve.

SERVES 4

150 g rice vermicelli

750 ml lobster stock (Better Than Bouillon Lobster Base, if available, otherwise fish stock cube)

2–3 tbsps ginger concentrate

2–3 tbsps soy sauce

Some lemon pepper

300 g crayfish meat

2 eggs

PREPARATION TIME:
approx. 20 minutes
570 kcal/2396 kJ

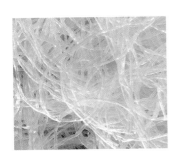

SPICY COCONUT CHICKEN BROTH

SERVES 4

1 onion
2 garlic cloves
1 red and 1 green chilli
1 lemon grass stem
1 piece fresh galangal
(approx. 1 cm)
1 tbsp groundnut oil
2 tsps red curry paste
3 kaffir lime leaves
500 ml chicken stock
300 ml coconut milk
250 ml cream
Some fish sauce
Some lime juice
600 g chicken breast fillets
125 g button mushrooms
2 tomatoes
3 spring onions
Some fresh coriander

PREPARATION TIME:
approx. 20 minutes (plus
cooking time)
390 kcal/1638 kJ

1 Peel and finely chop the onion and garlic. Wash and halve the chillies, remove the stalks and seeds, and chop finely.

2 Wash, trim and finely chop the lemon grass. Peel the galangal and chop it finely as well.

3 Fry all the vegetables in the groundnut oil with the curry paste in the wok. Add the washed lime leaves and pour in the chicken stock, then simmer for 15 minutes.

4 Add the coconut milk and cream to the mixture, stir well, and simmer for 5 minutes. Season to taste with fish sauce and lime juice.

5 Cut the chicken breast into strips. Brush the mushrooms clean and slice them.

6 Cover the tomatoes with boiling water for a few minutes, then remove the skins, seeds and chop them into small cubes. Wash, trim and finely chop the spring onions.

7 Add everything to the spicy mixture and cook for 5 minutes.

8 Wash the coriander, shake it dry, and pick the leaves from the stalks. Serve the chicken broth sprinkled with coriander leaves.

PRAWN AND GINGER SOUP

1 Soak the red chillies in hot water for 15 minutes. Drain, then whizz them in a blender with the onion, ginger, lemon grass, nuts, prawn paste, saffron and 2 tbsps oil.

2 De-vein the prawns and wash them. Brown the heads and shells in 1 tbsp oil until they turn dark orange. Add 750 ml water and simmer without a lid for 30 minutes. Remove from heat and strain off the stock.

3 Gently fry the spice paste in 1 tbsp oil in a wok for 6 minutes. Add the prawn stock and coconut milk and simmer for 5 minutes. Add the prawns and cook until they turn pink. Set aside a few cooked prawns for garnish. Strain the bean sprouts and heat up in the mixture.

4 Soak the noodles for 30 seconds in boiling water, drain and stir into the mixture. Serve the soup in bowls, garnished with a few cooked prawns and washed mint leaves.

SERVES 4

5 dried red chillies

2 small onions, chopped

2 tbsps freshly grated ginger

1 tbsp chopped lemon grass

8 kemiri (or macadamia) nuts

1½ tsps prawn paste

¼ tsp saffron powder

4 tbsps oil

600 g raw prawns

500 ml coconut milk

100 g bean sprouts

500 g fresh rice vermicelli

10 Korean mint leaves

PREPARATION TIME:
approx. 25 minutes (plus soaking and cooking time)
488 kcal/2048 kJ

COCONUT AND DUCK SOUP

SERVES 4

600 g duck breast fillet,
skin removed
3 garlic cloves
2 shallots
100 g oyster mushrooms
100 g runner beans
1 piece fresh ginger (3 cm)
1 piece fresh coriander root
(3 cm)
2 kaffir limes
1 lime
1 red pepper
3 tbsps groundnut oil
400 ml chicken stock
500 ml coconut milk
1 tbsp green curry paste
(jar or packet)
Thai basil for garnish

PREPARATION TIME:
approx. 50 minutes
657 kcal/2762 kJ

1 Wash and pat dry the duck meat then cut it into strips.

2 Peel and finely chop the garlic cloves. Peel and chop the shallots. Wash and trim the oyster mushrooms and chop them up.

3 Wash, dry, and finely chop the beans. Peel and grate the ginger.

4 Peel and slice the coriander root. Peel the kaffir limes and finely chop the peel. Then fillet the lime into segments.

5 Wash the pepper, cut it in half lengthways, remove the seeds and cut it into strips.

6 Heat the oil in a wok and brown the duck meat with the garlic and shallots for 4 minutes. Then add the mushrooms and beans.

7 Add the ginger, coriander root, kaffir lime, lime segments and pepper, and sauté briefly.

8 Pour in the chicken stock, coconut milk and approx. 300 ml water, and simmer gently for about 6 minutes. Season the mixture with curry paste.

9 Wash and pat dry the Thai basil leaves, then tear off the leaves. Ladle the soup into small bowls and serve garnished with basil.

WONTON SOUP

1 Drain the liquid from the mushrooms. Squeeze excess water out, remove the stems and finely chop the caps. Peel the prawns, de-vein, and chop them finely.

2 Thoroughly mix together the prawn meat, mushrooms, mince, salt, soy sauce, sesame oil, half of the spring onions, ginger, and water chestnuts.

3 Work with the wonton wrappers as quickly as possible, and cover the remaining wrappers with a damp cloth to prevent them from drying out.

4 Put 1 heaped teaspoon of the filling onto the middle of the wrapper. Damp the edges of the wrapper with water, fold into triangles, and press down the edges slightly. Lay the dumplings on a wooden board dusted with flour.

5 Bring a large pot of water to the boil. Cook the dumplings in fast-boiling water for 4–5 minutes. Bring the chicken stock to the boil in a separate pot, and add the rest of the finely chopped spring onions.

6 Remove the dumplings from the water with a skimmer, drain and keep them warm. Arrange the dumplings in small bowls or dishes and pour the boiling stock over them. Serve the soup immediately.

SERVES 4

3 dried Chinese mushrooms, soaked

200 g raw prawns

200 g pork mince

1 pinch salt

1 tbsp soy sauce

1 tsp sesame oil

5 finely chopped spring onions

1 piece freshly grated ginger (approx. 1 cm)

2 tbsps finely chopped water chestnuts

200 g wonton wrappers (pre-packed, from Asian grocers)

1 litre chicken stock

PREPARATION TIME:
approx. 40 minutes (plus cooking time)
243 kcal/1023 kJ

VEGETABLES

Freshness and simplicity are some of the basic principles of Asian cuisine, so it's logical that vegetables and aromatic herbs are also rated very highly. These ingredients can be cooked in a matter of minutes in a wok, without losing any of the flavour, vitamins or nutrients.

RICE WITH OMELETTE STRIPS

1 Wash and drain the rice, then cook it in about ½ litre water with a little added salt for about 15–20 minutes. Pour off the liquid and drain well.

2 Wash and trim the mushrooms, then chop them into smaller pieces, depending on the size. Wash the peas, drain the bamboo shoots, then peel and slice the carrots.

3 Heat 2 tbsps oil in a wok and lightly fry the mushrooms until all the liquid has evaporated. Add the vegetables and braise for 5 minutes until cooked but still firm to the bite. Set the wok aside.

4 Whisk the eggs in a bowl with a pinch of salt, then make them into an omelette in a frying pan. Lift the omelette out of the pan and cut into strips.

5 Mix the rice with the vegetables in the wok, heat up briefly, and season to taste with the sauces and tamarind juice. Divide the vegetable rice into dishes and garnish with the omelette strips. Serve sprinkled with chopped chives.

SERVES 4

350 g rice

Salt

250 g Chinese mu-err mushrooms

150 g peas

100 g bamboo shoots (tinned)

1 carrot

2 tbsps oil

4 eggs

2 tbsps soy sauce

2 tbsps oyster sauce

2 tbsps tamarind juice

3 tbsps chopped chives

PREPARATION TIME:
30 minutes (plus cooking, braising and frying time)
approx. 460 kcal/1932 kJ

PAK CHOI WITH EGG

SERVES 4

600–700 g pak choi

2 onions

4 chillies

3–4 tbsps groundnut oil

300 g chopped, tinned tomatoes

4–5 tbsps soy sauce

2–3 tbsps coconut milk

Salt

Freshly ground pepper

4–5 quail's eggs (cooked, in a jar)

PREPARATION TIME:
approx. 30 minutes
235 kcal/990 kJ

1 Wash and trim the pak choi, then drain well. Chop the vegetable into bite-size pieces. Peel and finely chop the onions. Slit the chillies lengthways, remove the seeds and membrane, and rinse them under running water. Finely chop the chillies.

2 Heat the oil in a wok, add the chopped onions and chillies, and gently stir-fry. Add the pak choi, braise it for a minute or two, and deglaze with the chopped tomato, soy sauce and coconut milk. Simmer for about 10–15 minutes. Season with salt and pepper.

3 Drain the eggs well and cut them in half. Arrange the vegetables in a serving dish, and garnish with eggs.

VEGETABLE MEDLEY

1 Peel and finely chop the onions and garlic. Wash and trim the aubergines and courgettes, cut them in half, first lengthways and then into wedges. Remove the skin from the tomatoes, halve them, scoop out the seeds and cut the flesh into small pieces. Cut the peppers in half, remove the seeds, wash them and cut them into fairly large chunks.

2 Heat the oil in the wok, and fry the vegetables separately for about 2–3 minutes, stirring continuously. Then mix all the vegetables together in the wok and season with salt, pepper, mustard seed and cumin.

3 Wash, trim and finely chop the herbs. Add to the vegetable mix and deglaze with vegetable stock. Cook for about 2–3 minutes. Dry roast the sesame seeds in a pan and sprinkle over the vegetables.

SERVES 4

3 red onions

2 garlic cloves

2 small aubergines and 2 small courgettes

4 beef tomatoes

2 peppers

4 tbsps sesame oil

Salt, freshly ground pepper, mustard seed and ground cumin

1–2 Thai basil stems

1–2 lemon grass stems

1 tbsp dried lemon grass

500 ml vegetable stock

2–3 tbsps sesame seeds, hulled

PREPARATION TIME:
approx. 25 minutes
480 kcal/2017 kJ

BUDDHIST FAST FOOD

SERVES 4

25 g dried morel mushrooms

200 g tofu

150 g Chinese cabbage, 100 g of both red and green pepper

125 g bamboo shoots

100 g carrots

100 g straw mushrooms

100 g button mushrooms

3 garlic cloves

5 tbsps oil

1 tbsp sugar, 2 tsps salt, pepper

300 ml vegetable stock

3 tbsps sesame oil

125 g bean sprouts

PREPARATION TIME:
approx. 30 minutes (plus soaking and cooking time) approx. 156 kcal/654 kJ

1 Soak the morels in hot water for 10 minutes. Then pour off the liquid and drain well.

2 Cut the tofu into cubes. Wash and trim the vegetables, then chop them into 3 cm pieces or slices. Wash and trim the mushrooms, and depending on their size, either cut them in half or leave them whole. Peel and finely chop the garlic.

3 Rub a little oil around the wok, then heat up the rest. Start by sweating the garlic briefly, and then add the vegetables gradually. Gently stir-fry for about 5 minutes.

4 Season to taste with sugar, salt, and pepper, and stir in the vegetable stock. Bring to the boil and stir well again. Finish off by drizzling with sesame oil. A meal you can eat on a fasting regime, to be served with rice.

DID YOU KNOW?

In Buddhism, fasting is not approached with the same degree of asceticism as in other world religions. The important thing is to live a harmonious, well-balanced life. Buddhist monks observe certain rites when it comes to food, so they do not eat any solid food after midday during the fasting period.

STEAMED COURGETTE TARTLETS

SERVES 4

3 large courgettes
1 bunch coriander
1 tbsp finely grated ginger
4 tbsps shrimp paste

PREPARATION TIME:
approx. 30 minutes
41 kcal/172 kJ

1 Wash, dry and trim the courgettes, then slice them very thinly. Wash the coriander and shake it dry, pick the leaves off the stalks, and finely chop a few of them. Mix the ginger with the shrimp paste and 2 tbsps water.

2 Line bamboo steamers with a few coriander leaves. Brush the courgette slices with some paste, and layer on top of each other to make tartlets (approx. 5 cm high).

3 Place the courgette tartlets in the bamboo steamers, and sprinkle with chopped coriander leaves.

4 Heat up water in the wok, and place the steamers on a rack over the water. Cover wok with a lid and steam for about 15 minutes.

DID YOU KNOW?

Coriander is also known as "Chinese parsley" – but although the two plants may look the same, they taste completely different.

TOMATOES WITH GINGER CABBAGE

1 Wash and dry the tomatoes, cut off the tops, and scoop out the insides. Remove the bitter outside leaves of the cabbage, cut it in half, remove the stalk, and chop the leaves into thin strips. Peel and thinly slice the ginger.

2 Heat the oil in the wok, add the cabbage strips, and braise with the ground ginger, hoisin sauce and fish sauce until soft. Stuff the tomatoes with the cabbage strips. Put three tomatoes in each bamboo steamer and sprinkle with ginger slices.

3 Heat some water in the wok, and layer the steamers on top of a rack. Cover the wok with a lid. After 10 minutes, swap the top baskets with the lower ones and steam for a further 10 minutes.

4 Finally, drizzle a little coriander oil over the tomatoes and sprinkle with finely chopped coriander leaves.

SERVES 4

12 medium-size tomatoes
½ small white cabbage
100 g root ginger
1 tbsp vegetable oil
2 tbsps ground ginger
1 tbsp hoisin sauce
2 tbsps fish sauce
Some coriander oil
½ bunch coriander

PREPARATION TIME:
approx. 40 minutes
122 kcal/512 kJ

BAMBOO SHOOTS WITH ALFALFA

SERVES 4

500 g bamboo shoots
2 red and 2 green peppers
1 sprig of coriander
4 tbsps vegetable oil
1 tbsp shrimp paste
2 tbsps hoisin sauce
100 g alfalfa sprouts

PREPARATION TIME:
approx. 25 minutes
146 kcal/611 kJ

1 Slice the bamboo shoots on the diagonal. Wash, trim, and dry the peppers, then cut them into strips. Wash the coriander, shake it dry, pick the leaves off the stalks, and finely chop them.

2 Heat the oil in the wok, sauté the pepper strips and then add the bamboo shoots. Add the shrimp paste and hoisin sauce; mix well, and continue to stir-fry it.

3 When cooked, mix in the alfalfa sprouts, toss them briefly, and serve with sprinkled coriander leaves.

FRIED SHIITAKE MUSHROOMS

SERVES 4

600 g fresh shiitake
mushrooms
1 bunch spring onions
4 tbsps roasted sesame oil
1 tbsp sesame seeds
2 tbsps oyster sauce
4 tbsps rice wine

PREPARATION TIME:
approx. 15 minutes
183 kcal/767 kJ

1 Instead of washing
them, just wipe the
shiitake mushrooms clean
with kitchen roll. Remove the
bottom of the stalks only.

2 Wash, trim and dry the
spring onions, then cut
them on the round.

3 Heat the sesame oil in
the wok, and sear the
mushrooms until cooked.
Then add the chopped spring
onion and fry for another
few minutes. Sprinkle on the

sesame seeds and lightly
roast them.

4 Add the oyster sauce and
deglaze with rice wine.
Cook briefly, just enough to
evaporate the liquid.

SPINACH WITH ROASTED GARLIC

1 Trim and wash the spinach well under running water, then gently shake it dry.

2 Peel the garlic cloves and cut them into thin strips.

3 Heat the oil in the wok, and gently fry the garlic until pale golden. Add the bean sprouts and toss briefly.

4 Add the spinach and wilt it down. Season with fish sauce and serve.

SERVES 4

1 kg fresh spinach leaves
5 garlic cloves
3 tbsps groundnut oil
500 g bean sprouts
2 tbsps fish sauce

PREPARATION TIME:
approx. 15 minutes
180 kcal/754 kJ

TIP

Healthy bean sprouts taste best when eaten fresh. If need be, you can also resort to a tin or jar.

63

COURGETTE FRITTERS

SERVES 4

800 g courgettes
125 g ground cashew nuts
50 g grated Parmesan cheese
½ bunch coriander
1 egg
A pinch of salt
Pepper
60 ml groundnut oil
400 g sour cream
100 g natural yoghurt
1 garlic clove
1 small red pepper
Ground ginger and ground cumin

PREPARATION TIME:
approx. 30 minutes
816 kcal/3430 kJ

1 Wash and dry the courgettes, then cut them lengthways into thin slices. Mix the cashew nuts and cheese. Wash, dry and finely chop the coriander leaves and stir into the cheese mix.

2 Whisk the egg in a bowl and season with salt and pepper. Firstly, dip the courgette slices in the egg and then in the cheese mix. Lightly press on the coating.

3 Heat the oil in the wok and fry the courgette slices until golden brown.

4 Mix the sour cream and yoghurt in a bowl. Add the peeled and crushed garlic. Wash the pepper, cut it in half and remove the seeds, then chop it very finely and mix into the dip. Season with salt, pepper, ground ginger and ground cumin. Serve the courgette fritters with the dip.

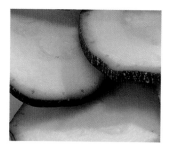  

ENDIVE FRITTERS

1 Trim and wash the endives under running water, then drain well. Dry the leaves and cut them into pieces about 5 cm long.

2 Whisk the egg white until stiff. Beat the yolks and fold them into the whisked whites. Fold in the salt, flour and cornflour. Dip the endive leaves in the batter and deep-fry in hot groundnut oil until golden brown.

3 To make the first sauce, heat the orange juice, remove from the stove, and stir in the groundnut oil, paprika, chilli powder and coriander leaves.

4 To make the second sauce, warm up the soy sauce and add the five-spice powder and sugar. Stir over heat until the sugar has dissolved.

5 For the third sauce, mix the vinegar with the sesame oil, sugar and a little salt. Trim, wash and finely chop the spring onions, then stir them into the sauce.

6 Put the three sauces into bowls and arrange the well-drained endive fritters on a plate to serve.

SERVES 4

500 g endives
8 egg whites
2 egg yolks
A pinch of salt
2 tbsps flour
1 tbsp cornflour
Groundnut oil for frying
100 ml orange juice
1 tbsp each of groundnut oil and ground paprika
1 tsp chilli powder
20 g coriander leaves
100 ml light soy sauce
1 tbsp five-spice powder
2–3 tbsps sugar
100 ml raspberry vinegar
1 tsp each of sesame oil and sugar
¼ bunch spring onions

PREPARATION TIME:
approx. 30 minutes
367 kcal/1541 kJ

SPRING ROLLS

SERVES 4

4 eggs
1 pinch salt
2 tbsps oil
200 g flour
Butter for frying
1 large onion
3 garlic cloves
1 tin of bamboo shoots
(approx. 200 g)
2 carrots
100 g bean sprouts

PREPARATION TIME:
approx. 30 minutes
(plus resting time)
303 kcal/1271 kJ

1 To make the batter, separate 1 egg and put the yolk to one side. Whisk the egg white with the remaining eggs and about 350 ml water. Add salt, oil and flour, mixing everything to a smooth batter. Allow it to rest for 30 minutes.

2 Heat a knob of butter in the wok until it foams and make very thin, light pancakes with the batter, one at a time. Set them aside on a plate as you make them.

3 To make the filling, peel and finely chop the onion and garlic. Drain and thinly slice the bamboo shoots. Peel the carrots and thinly slice them as well. Wash the bean sprouts.

4 Heat a knob of butter in the wok. Sweat the garlic and onion in it. Add the carrots and fry it all for 3 minutes. Add the bean sprouts and fry for another 2 minutes.

5 Fill the pancakes with the vegetable mix. Roll them up tightly and brush with the beaten egg yolk. Fry the rolls in a little butter, turning them until golden brown all over.

SWEET-AND-SOUR PEPPERS

1 Wash, trim and remove the seeds from the peppers, then cut them into thin strips. Cut across the tomatoes at the stem, dip them in boiling water for a minute or two, plunge them into cold water, remove the skins, and cut them into sections.

2 Peel and crush the garlic cloves. Wash, dry and finely chop the parsley. Heat the oil in the wok and sweat the vegetables in it. Pour in the rice wine and soy sauce.

3 Leave it to rest for a few minutes, then season to taste with the sugar, ground aniseed, coriander and ginger. Spoon onto plates and serve.

SERVES 4

2 red, 2 yellow and 2 green peppers

4 tomatoes

6 garlic cloves

½ bunch parsley

3 tbsps groundnut oil

4 tbsps rice wine

4 tbsps soy sauce

1 tbsp sugar

Ground aniseed, ground coriander and ground ginger

PREPARATION TIME:

approx. 20 minutes
255 kcal/1072 kJ

  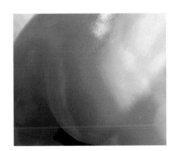

THAI VEGETABLES

SERVES 4

125 g broccoli
125 g cauliflower
½ cucumber
3 carrots
125 g Chinese cabbage
125 g pak choi
100 g tinned sweetcorn
500 ml rice vinegar
2 tbsps sugar
Salt
5 garlic cloves
2 onions
6 dried red chillies
75 ml groundnut oil
2 tbsps sesame seeds

PREPARATION TIME:
approx. 35 minutes
319 kcal/1340 kJ

1 Wash, trim and dry the vegetables, then chop them into small pieces. Drain the sweetcorn well in a sieve. Bring the vinegar, 500 ml water, sugar and a pinch of salt to the boil. Blanch the vegetables in it in batches.

2 Peel and roughly chop the garlic and onions. Pound them finely in a mortar along with the chillies. Heat the oil in the wok and fry the paste for about 3 minutes.

3 Add the vegetables and their cooking water and braise on a low heat for about 2 minutes. Dry-roast the sesame seeds in a pan.

4 Arrange the vegetables on plates and serve sprinkled with sesame seeds.

TIP

The great thing about this recipe is that you can experiment with different types of vegetable according to taste and season. Romanesco, spinach, courgettes, pumpkin and runner beans are worth a try, or it's even delicious with fresh mushrooms.

SWEET GARLIC AUBERGINES

1 Wash the aubergines and trim off the stems, then cut them in half lengthways. Cut the halves into chunks measuring about 3 × 3 cm.

2 Heat 3 tbsps of the oil in a wok, turning carefully to distribute the oil all over. Put half of the aubergine chunks in the wok, and stir-fry them for 5 minutes until browned and the oil is completely absorbed.

3 Drain the aubergines on kitchen roll. Stir-fry the rest of the aubergines in 3 tbsps oil, remove them from the wok and drain them.

4 Heat the remaining oil in the wok. Peel and finely chop the garlic and onion, then fry for 3 minutes in the hot oil. Sprinkle the sugar on them and lightly caramelise them. Add the soy sauce, vinegar, and sherry, and boil it all up, stirring continuously.

5 Put the fried aubergine chunks back in the wok and cook for another 3 minutes until the sauce is almost absorbed. Serve the aubergines with white rice.

SERVES 4

4 small aubergines
7 tbsps oil
3–4 garlic cloves
1 onion
6 tsps brown sugar
6 tsps soy sauce
6 tsps apple vinegar
1 tbsp dry sherry

PREPARATION TIME:
approx. 10 minutes
(plus cooking time)
77 kcal/323 kJ

SWEET-AND-SOUR VEGETABLES

SERVES 4

100 g Chinese cabbage
125 g carrots
125 g fresh shiitake
mushrooms
125 g mangetout
50 g ginger
2 garlic cloves
2 red chillies
100 g tinned bamboo shoots
150 g pineapple
4 tbsps sunflower oil
4 tbsps rice vinegar
4 tbsps light soy sauce
4 tbsps sherry
2 tbsps sugar
200 ml chicken stock
1 tsp cornflour

PREPARATION TIME:
approx. 30 minutes
399 kcal/1676 kJ

1 Wash and dry the Chinese cabbage, and cut the leaves in half lengthways. Then cut them into 2 cm strips.

2 Peel and thinly slice the carrots. Wipe the mushrooms clean with kitchen roll and cut them in half.

3 Wash the mangetout and cut them in half. Peel the ginger and slice it very thinly.

4 Peel and finely chop the garlic. Wash and de-seed the chillies, then cut them into thin strips.

5 Drain the bamboo shoots in a sieve. Peel the pineapple, remove the stalk, and cut the flesh into pieces.

6 Heat the oil in the wok and fry the carrots, mushrooms, mangetout and Chinese cabbage.

7 Add the ginger, garlic and chilli, and fry briefly. Add the bamboo shoots, pineapple, vinegar, soy sauce, sherry and sugar. Pour in ¾ of the stock and mix well.

8 Mix the cornflour with the remaining cold stock and pour over the vegetables, mixing well. Simmer for 4 minutes.

9 Arrange the mixture in small bowls and serve with rice.

SCRAMBLED EGG WITH MUSHROOMS

1 Soak the dried mushrooms in enough hot water to cover them completely. Leave for about 15 minutes.

2 Wash and de-seed the chilli, then cut it into thin strips. Peel and finely chop the ginger. Wash and trim the spring onions, then cut them on the round. Wash and dry the coriander, and pick off the leaves.

3 Drain the mushrooms in a sieve and chop them up. Whisk the eggs, then stir in the soy sauce, pepper and groundnut oil.

4 Heat the wok and add the sunflower oil. Sauté the mushrooms. Add the rest of the ingredients, except the eggs and coriander, and mix well with the mushrooms. Pour in the egg mix and cook it until it starts to thicken. As it sets, push the cooked egg mix out towards the sides of the wok.

5 Arrange the scrambled egg on a dish and sprinkle with coriander leaves.

SERVES 4

3 dried morel mushrooms
3 dried shiitake mushrooms
1 red chilli
10 g ginger
2 spring onions
2 stems of coriander
4 eggs
2 tsps soy sauce
A pinch of pepper
1 tsp groundnut oil
2 tbsps sunflower oil

PREPARATION TIME:
approx. 30 minutes
230 kcal/966 kJ

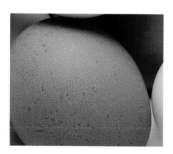

BEAN SPROUTS WITH ORANGE

SERVES 4

250 g bean sprouts
250 g mixed pickles (a jar)
3–4 tbsps sesame oil
2–3 oranges
250 g smoked tofu
Salt
Freshly ground pepper
4 tbsps soy sauce
1 carton of cress

PREPARATION TIME:
approx. 20 minutes
248 kcal/1042 kJ

1 Rinse the bean sprouts briefly under cold running water. Drain well in a sieve. Also drain the mixed pickles.

2 Heat the oil in the wok and quickly stir-fry the vegetables. Peel and segment the oranges, removing all the pith. Use a sharp knife to fillet the orange into segments and then chop it into small pieces.

3 Cut the tofu into cubes. Add the tofu and orange segments to the vegetables and season it all with salt, pepper and soy sauce. Simmer for about 2 minutes.

4 Wash and dry the cress, and cut off the soil. Serve the food in small bowls, garnished with cress.

SICHUAN CUCUMBER WITH BULGUR

SERVES 4

2 medium cucumbers
1 bunch spring onions
1 piece of fresh ginger
(4 cm)
2 garlic cloves
1 red chilli
3–4 tbsps sesame oil
1 tbsp sugar
2–3 tbsps soy sauce
1–2 tsps Sichuan pepper
1 tbsp chilli oil
150 g bulgur

PREPARATION TIME:

approx. 25 minutes
313 kcal/1315 kJ

1 Wash and halve the cucumbers. Remove the seeds and cut them into slices on the diagonal. Wash and trim the spring onions, then cut them thinly on the round.

2 Peel and finely chop the ginger and garlic cloves. Wash, de-seed, and finely chop the chilli.

3 Heat the oil and stir-fry the vegetables for about 6–7 minutes. Add the sugar, soy sauce and Sichuan pepper. Next add the chilli oil.

4 Simmer for another 6–8 minutes. In the meantime prepare the bulgur according to the instructions on the packet. Carefully mix the bulgur into the other ingredients in the wok, and serve in small bowls.

AUBERGINES IN YOGHURT SAUCE

1 Wash, trim, and slice the aubergine lengthways. Sprinkle with salt and leave for about 30 minutes.

2 Dry-roast the poppy and cumin seeds in a small pan on a medium heat until you can smell the aroma. Then grind them.

3 Mix the yoghurt with 250 ml cold water. Finely chop the chillies. Melt the butter in a pan and briefly sweat the chillies and fennel seeds.

4 Squeeze all the liquid out of the aubergine and fry in butter for about 5 minutes until pale brown. Add the thinned yogurt and simmer for about 10 minutes on a medium heat until the aubergine is soft.

5 When the sauce has reduced a little, mix in the roasted spices and the sugar. Goes well with baked potatoes.

SERVES 4

1 aubergine (approx. 250 g)
1½ tsps salt
½ tsp black poppy seeds
1 tsp cumin seeds
150 g natural yoghurt
2 dried red chillies
2 tbsps butter
1 tsp fennel seeds
1 tsp sugar

PREPARATION TIME:
25 minutes (plus soaking and cooking time)
approx. 70 kcal/293 kJ

RICE AND NOODLES

No dish is served without rice or noodles in Asia. It doesn't matter whether you are making an easy everyday meal or planning a lavish feast, rice and noodle dishes are more than just simple accompaniments when combined with the best Asian flavours and fine ingredients. Check it out for yourself!

RICE WITH PORK FILLET

SERVES 4

100–150 g rice

750 ml veal stock (or beef if unavailable)

250 ml chicken stock

2–3 tbsps soy sauce

2–3 tbsps rice wine

250 g pork fillet

1 bunch spring onions

2–3 tbsps sesame oil

200 g green asparagus (from a jar)

Salt, pepper

Ground ginger and garlic powder

½ tub of cress

PREPARATION TIME:
approx. 35 minutes
370 kcal/1555 kJ

1 Put the rice in a sieve and blanch with hot water. Mix the stocks, soy sauce and rice wine. Put this mixture into a pan along with the rice and bring to the boil. Simmer on a low heat for about 15–20 minutes.

2 Wash the pork fillet, pat it dry, and cut it into thin strips. Wash, trim and cut the spring onions on the round.

3 Heat the oil in the wok and stir-fry the pork and spring onions for about 4–5 minutes. Drain the asparagus well in a sieve. Cut it into bite-size pieces and combine it with the meat in the wok. Heat up the mixture and season to taste with the spices.

4 Mix the meat and asparagus with the rice and serve in small bowls, sprinkled with cress.

RICE WITH CHICKEN BREAST

SERVES 4

250 g short-grain rice
300 ml chicken stock
5 tbsps rice wine
5 tbsps soy sauce
2 stems of lemon grass
2 tbsps five-spice powder
4 baby turnips
200 g runner beans
5 tbsps sesame oil
2 chicken breasts, sliced
200 g bitter melon
3 tbsps pine nut kernels
4 tbsps duck sauce (packet)

PREPARATION TIME:
approx. 40 minutes (plus
cooking time)
632 kcal/2656 kJ

1 Dry-roast the rice in a pan. Grind it in a blender when it has cooled down, but not too finely.

2 Heat up the stock, rice wine and soy sauce. Wash, trim and finely chop the lemon grass and mix in the five-spice powder. Peel and dice the baby turnips. Wash, trim and finely chop the beans. Add all of these ingredients to the boiling stock and simmer for about 7 minutes. Lift out the vegetables and drain them.

3 Heat the oil in the wok and brown the chicken. Dice the bitter melon and add to the chicken along with the vegetables and pine nuts. Fry for 3 minutes. Stir in the rice and season to taste with duck sauce.

DID YOU KNOW?

The composition of five-spice powder varies from country to country. Its basic ingredients are fennel seeds, cloves, cardamom, star anise, and cinnamon.

FRIED RICE WITH CHICKEN

1 Peel and finely chop the garlic. Wash and trim the spring onions, then cut them on the round. Wash the cucumber and cut it into strips. Skin and finely dice the tomatoes.

2 Heat the oil in a wok and gently fry the chicken until cooked. Remove it from the wok and keep it warm.

3 Beat the eggs and fry in the cooking oil, stirring continuously. Add the rice, garlic and chicken, and heat it up, stirring continuously.

4 Stir in the fish sauce, pepper and sugar. Put the rice mixture in a dish, and serve garnished with spring onions, cucumber strips and diced tomato.

SERVES 4

2–3 garlic cloves

8 spring onions

½ cucumber

5 tomatoes

3 tbsps oil

200 g chicken breast, sliced

3 eggs

400 g steamed jasmine rice

3 tbsps fish sauce

White pepper

1 tbsp sugar

PREPARATION TIME:
approx. 15 minutes
(plus cooking time)
568 kcal/2384 kJ

KOREAN NOODLES WITH VEGETABLES

1 Pour boiling water over the black mushrooms and leave to soak for 10 minutes. Drain well.

2 Cook the noodles in boiling water according to the packet instructions. Drain and rinse well under cold water until they have cooled completely. This removes the excess starch. Cut the noodles to the length you prefer.

3 Peel and finely chop the garlic and ginger. Wash, trim and finely chop all but two of the spring onions – cut these into pieces about 5 cm long. Peel the carrots and cut them into long, thin strips.

4 Heat 1 tbsp sesame oil and the vegetable oil in the wok. Stir-fry the garlic, ginger and the 4 finely chopped spring onions for 3 minutes on a medium heat. Wash and trim the pak choi, drain well, and chop it into small pieces.

5 Add the carrot strips and fry for 1 minute. Add the drained noodles, the remaining spring onions, pak choi, the rest of the sesame oil, soy sauce, mirin and sugar. Mix it all together, cover with a lid, and simmer for 2 minutes. Add the mushrooms, cover again, and cook for another 2 minutes. Sprinkle with sesame and seaweed powder, and serve immediately.

SERVES 4

4 tbsps dried black mushrooms

300 g Korean noodles

3 garlic cloves

1 piece of fresh ginger (approx. 5 cm)

6 spring onions

3 carrots

3 tbsps sesame oil

2 tbsps vegetable oil

500 g pak choi or 250 g spinach

60 ml Japanese soy sauce

2 tbsps mirin

1 tsp sugar

2 tbsps sesame and seaweed powder

PREPARATION TIME:
approx. 30 minutes (plus soaking and cooking time)
260 kcal/1092 kJ

RICE BALLS WITH SHRIMPS

SERVES 4

200 g basmati rice
200 g shelled shrimps
2 tbsps fish sauce (bottle)
½ tsp finely grated ginger
1 tsp chilli flakes
For the dip:
6 tbsps fish sauce
Juice of 1 lime
3 finely chopped red chillies
1 tbsp finely chopped
coriander

PREPARATION TIME:
approx. 35 minutes
174 kcal/729 kJ

1 Cook the basmati rice according to the packet instructions and leave to cool. To make the filling, mix together the shrimps, fish sauce and finely grated ginger. With damp hands, form little balls of rice, press a dent in the middle, add some filling and close over again into a ball. Make 12 balls this way.

2 Place the balls in bamboo steamers and sprinkle with chilli flakes. Boil some water in the wok, place the steamers on a rack over the water, and cover the wok with a lid.

3 After 15 minutes, swap the top steamers with the bottom ones. Steam for another 15 minutes. To make the dip, mix together the fish sauce, lime juice, chillies and coriander.

RICE WITH SHIITAKE MUSHROOMS

1 Cook the rice according to the packet instructions and set aside. Soak the mushrooms in water. Cut the peppers into bite-size pieces. Cut the spring onions in half lengthways, then chop them up.

2 Heat the oil in the wok and start by frying the spring onions. Then add the peppers and continue to stir-fry for a minute or two.

3 If necessary, cut the drained shiitake mushrooms into smaller pieces, add to the vegetables and fry again. Season with soy and fish sauces. Finally mix in the cooked rice and stir-fry the mixture until the rice is piping hot.

SERVES 4

250 g long-grain rice
200 g dried shiitake mushrooms
2 red peppers
1 bunch spring onions
4 tbsps vegetable oil
2 tbsps light soy sauce
2 tbsps fish sauce

PREPARATION TIME:
approx. 25 minutes
365 kcal/1527 kJ

TIP

You can also try this dish with sliced carrot instead of red peppers.

93

GINGER RICE BALLS

1 Cook the basmati rice according to the packet instructions and leave it to cool.

2 Peel and slice the ginger, and finely chop the coriander. Peel and finely chop 3 shallots, fry in hot oil until crispy, then remove from the wok.

3 Mix it all together with the preserved ginger and some coriander leaves to make the filling.

4 Line the bamboo steamers with coriander and ginger. With damp hands, form the cooked rice into balls; make a dent in the middle of each, fill it with the mixture, and close it over into a ball again.

5 Place the balls in the bamboo steamers, slice the remaining shallot, and strew it on top.

6 Heat up some water in the wok, place the bamboo steamers on a rack over the water, cover with a lid, and steam for 10 minutes.

7 Drizzle some sweet-and-sour sauce over the balls and serve the rest as a dip.

SERVES 4

200 g basmati rice
100 g root ginger
1 bunch coriander
4 shallots
2 tbsps vegetable oil
2 tbsps chopped preserved ginger
6 tbsps sweet-and-sour sauce (ready-made)

PREPARATION TIME:
approx. 40 minutes
207 kcal/866 kJ

STIR-FRIED RICE NOODLES

SERVES 4

400 ml chicken stock
300 g thin rice noodles
500 g tofu
3 red chillies
3 tbsps sesame oil
2 stems of lemon grass
1 piece fresh ginger (1 cm)
8 shallots
3 kaffir lime leaves
3 tbsps tomato juice
3 tbsps fish sauce
(ready-made)
2 tbsps palm sugar
2 tbsps lemon juice

PREPARATION TIME:
approx. 35 minutes
338 kcal/1421 kJ

1 Heat up the stock and soak the rice noodles in it for about 10 minutes. Dice the tofu. Wash the chillies, slice them down the middle, de-seed them and cut them into rings. Heat the oil in the wok and gently sauté the tofu and chillies.

2 Wash and dry the lemon grass, then add it to the wok. Peel and grate the ginger. Peel the shallots, dice them and add to the tofu along with the ginger. Wash, dry and finely chop the kaffir lime leaves. Add the lime leaves, tomato juice, fish sauce, palm sugar and lemon juice.

3 Mix together the rice noodles and tofu. Divide it between small bowls and serve.

THREAD NOODLES WITH MUSHROOMS

SERVES 4

100 g mung bean vermicelli
1 red and 1 yellow pepper
3–4 hot chillies
300 g oyster mushrooms
3 garlic cloves
1 piece fresh ginger (2 cm)
6–7 tbsps sesame oil
Salt, pepper, mustard powder
1 tbsp chilli sauce
125 ml mushroom stock (ready-made or stock cube)

PREPARATION TIME:
approx. 25 minutes
289 kcal/1215 kJ

1 Soak the noodles in warm water until soft. Drain well and cut into 3–4 cm lengths.

2 Cut the peppers and chillies in half, de-seed and wash them, then finely dice them. Wash and chop the mushrooms. Peel and finely chop the garlic and ginger.

3 Heat the oil in the wok and stir-fry all the vegetables in separate batches for about 3–4 minutes. Add the noodles and stir-fry for about 1 minute.

4 Season with the spices and add the chilli sauce and mushroom stock. Cook over a medium heat for about 4–5 minutes. Arrange the noodles in bowls with the mushrooms and vegetables, and serve.

NOODLES WITH VEGETABLES AND CRAB

1 Soak the noodles in a bowl of warm water for 10 minutes. Then rinse and drain well. Peel and slice the carrot. Wash and trim the pak choi and celery and cut them into same-size strips.

2 Heat the oil in a wok. Peel and finely chop the garlic. Sweat it gently in the hot oil, then add the carrot slices and fry them briefly as well. Mix in the pak choi and celery and cook for a further 2 minutes.

3 Drain the crabmeat and add to the vegetables in the wok along with the noodles. Add the remaining ingredients and mix well. Stir-fry for another 2 minutes then serve.

SERVES 4

100 g rice vermicelli
1 carrot*
50 g pak choi*
½ head of celery*
2 tbsps sesame oil
1 garlic clove
100 g crabmeat, tinned*
3 tbsps vegetable stock
1 tbsp oyster sauce*
1 tbsp kecap manis (Indonesian sweet soy sauce)*
1 tsp sugar, pepper

PREPARATION TIME:
25 minutes (plus soaking and cooking time)
approx. 115 kcal/482 kJ

TIP

Asterisked ingredients can be substituted with an alternative. Spices and herbs can be added according to taste.

FOUR-COLOUR RICE

SERVES 4

500 g rice, salt

For the green rice:
2–3 tbsps sesame oil
100 g leaf spinach (frozen)
100 g peas (frozen)
125 ml vegetable stock
2–3 tbsps soy sauce
Pepper, onion and garlic powder, nutmeg

For the purple rice:
300 g beetroot (jar)
Ground cardamom and ground cloves

For the orange rice:
200 g sweet-sour pickled pumpkin
2 bananas
2–3 tinned apricots
2–3 tbsps sesame oil
1–2 tbsps yellow curry paste

For the red rice:
300 g chopped tomatoes with chilli, onion and garlic (pre-packed)
4–5 tbsps paprika paste
Pepper, sugar
2–3 tbsps sesame oil

PREPARATION TIME:
approx. 40 minutes
700 kcal/2941 kJ

1 Cook the rice in plenty of boiling salted water according to the packet instructions. Drain well.

2 To make the green rice: heat the sesame oil in the wok and sauté the roughly chopped spinach and the peas. Add the vegetable stock and soy sauce and cook for about 3–5 minutes on a low heat. Season to taste with salt, pepper, onion and garlic powder, and nutmeg. Carefully fold in a quarter of the cooked rice. Remove the mixture and keep it warm.

3 To make the purple rice: drain the beetroot well in a sieve, retaining the liquid, and dice it finely. Add to the wok with the liquid and heat up. Season with ground cardamom and cloves, then mix in another quarter of the rice. Remove the mixture and keep it warm.

4 To make the orange rice: drain the pumpkin well in a sieve and then dice it finely. Peel the bananas and dice them finely. Drain and finely chop the apricots. Heat the sesame oil and stir-fry the pumpkin, banana and apricot cubes for 1–2 minutes. Season the mixture with curry paste and carefully fold in a quarter of the rice. Remove the mixture and keep it warm.

5 To make the red rice: mix the chopped tomatoes with the paprika paste, salt, pepper, and sugar. Heat the sesame oil in the wok and heat up the tomato mix for 1–2 minutes, stirring continuously. Mix in the remaining rice and heat it up. Arrange the four different colours of rice in domes on plates and serve.

EGG NOODLES WITH SMALL PRAWNS

SERVES 4

250 g Chinese egg noodles

Salt

300 g mangetout

1 bunch spring onions

2 small, mild green chillies

2 tbsps sesame oil

250 g small prawns

2 tbsps light soy sauce

2 tbsps sweet-sour chilli sauce

6 eggs

PREPARATION TIME:
approx. 35 minutes
562 kcal/2355 kJ

1 Cook the egg noodles in salted water according to the packet instructions. Nip off the ends of the mangetout, wash and dry them, and cut them in half. Wash and trim the spring onions and cut them finely on the round. Wash, dry and chop the chillies into thin strips.

2 Heat the sesame oil in the wok and fry the spring onions. Stir in the mangetout and then the chilli strips. Finally, mix in the noodles and fry for another 3 minutes.

3 Add the prawns and season with soy sauce and chilli sauce. Push the noodle mix to the side and pour the whisked egg into the middle of the wok. Stir as it sets, and then mix in with the fried noodles.

NOODLES WITH LEAF SPINACH IN SOY SYRUP

1 Peel the pumpkin, remove the seeds and cut the flesh into strips.

2 Trim the spinach, rinse thoroughly under running water, and shake it dry.

3 Cook the rice noodles in boiling water, stirring to separate them. Drain, then plunge them briefly into cold water and drain again.

4 Heat the oil in the wok and fry the pumpkin strips. Deglaze with honey and soy sauce, and reduce it to a syrupy consistency.

5 Next add the cooked rice noodles and spinach, mixing carefully, and heat it up.

6 Cook the spinach until just wilted. Serve sprinkled with sesame seeds.

SERVES 4

600 g pumpkin
100 g fresh leaf spinach
250 g broad rice noodles
4 tbsps vegetable oil
2 tbsps honey
8 tbsps soy sauce
2 tbsps sesame seeds

PREPARATION TIME:
approx. 25 minutes
342 kcal/1431 kJ

  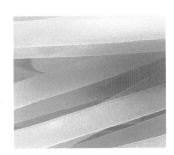

DEEP-FRIED GLASS NOODLES

SERVES 4

400 g parsnips
½ bunch spring onions
300 g mangetout
3–4 tbsps groundnut oil
Salt
Pepper
Nutmeg
Mustard powder
3–4 tbsps maple syrup
2–3 tbsps Dijon mustard
Groundnut oil for
deep-frying
120 g glass noodles

PREPARATION TIME:
approx. 30 minutes
435 kcal/1828 kJ

1 Peel the parsnips and cut them into small cubes. Wash, trim and dry the spring onions and cut them into pieces about 2–5 cm long. Wash, trim and drain the mangetout well.

2 Heat the oil in the wok and stir-fry the vegetables in separate batches for about 3–4 minutes. Season with the spices, remove from the wok and drain well.

3 Stir the maple syrup and mustard into the remaining frying oil in the wok, and heat up gently. Put the vegetables back in the wok and glaze them. Remove from the pan and keep them warm.

4 Clean the wok and add enough groundnut oil for deep-frying. Deep-fry the glass noodles in batches until crispy. Arrange the vegetables and glass noodles in a dish and serve.

TIP

As an alternative to parsnips you could use the same amount of celeriac or even parsley root.

106

YOGHURT RICE WITH LENTILS

1 Cook the rice and lentils in the vegetable stock for about 20 minutes. Season with salt, pepper, ground coriander and ginger.

2 Heat the butter in the wok. Add the well-drained pearl onions and stir-fry for 4–5 minutes.

3 Sieve the rice and lentil mix, draining well. Add to the pearl onions.

4 Season with ground cumin and cloves. Add the vinegar and cook on a gentle heat for about 3–5 minutes.

5 Carefully fold in the yoghurt, spoon into bowls, and serve immediately.

SERVES 4

100 g brown rice

50 g small green Puy lentils

500 ml vegetable stock (ready-made or stock cube)

Salt, pepper

Ground coriander and ground ginger

60 g pepper butter

100 g pearl onions (jar)

Ground cumin and cloves

1 tbsp raspberry vinegar

4–5 tbsps natural yoghurt

PREPARATION TIME:
approx. 30 minutes
298 kcal/1253 kJ

RICE VERMICELLI WITH CORIANDER SALSA

SERVES 4

250 g rice vermicelli
2 red and 2 yellow peppers
6 coriander leaves
4 tbsps vegetable oil
4 tbsps fish sauce
2 tbsps honey
2 tbsps white rice vinegar

PREPARATION TIME:
approx. 25 minutes
229 kcal/957 kJ

1 Cook the rice vermicelli according to the packet instructions. Drain, plunge briefly in cold water, and drain in a sieve.

2 Wash, trim, de-seed and dice the peppers. Chop the coriander leaves into fine strips.

3 Heat the oil in the wok, then sear the peppers and coriander leaves quickly in it. The peppers should still be *al dente*.

4 Add the cooked rice vermicelli, deglaze with the fish sauce, honey and rice vinegar, tossing it briefly, then serve immediately.

POULTRY

Peking duck is renowned all over the world as the classic poultry dish of Asia. Our aim in this chapter is to show you that Asian cuisine has far more to offer than this speciality. Discover delicious wok recipes using chicken, turkey, duck, guinea fowl, goose or pheasant. Whether it's braised, deep-fried, or marinated in a spicy paste – the diverse ways of cooking poultry are surpassed only by the enjoyment of eating it.

GUINEA FOWL NIBBLES

SERVES 4

600 g guinea fowl breast fillets

3–4 tbsps lemon pepper

150 g gram flour

2–3 tsps oil

1 tsp ground cumin

¼ tsp ground coriander

¼ tsp cayenne pepper

1 pinch salt

Groundnut oil for deep-frying

1 bunch mint

1 lemon balm

200 g natural yoghurt

2 tbsps double cream

Ground allspice, garlic powder and mustard powder

Pepper

½ head of lollo rosso lettuce

PREPARATION TIME:
approx. 30 minutes
(plus resting time)
716 kcal/3010 kJ

1 Cut the guinea fowl into thin strips. Season with lemon pepper and let it soak in for about 10–15 minutes. Mix the flour with the oil, spices and 50 ml water. Heat enough groundnut oil in the wok for deep-frying.

2 Dip the meat strips in the batter and fry in the hot oil until golden brown. Wash, dry and finely chop the herbs. Stir the yoghurt and double cream until smooth.

Fold in the herbs and season with allspice, garlic powder, mustard powder, salt and pepper.

3 Wash and dry the lettuce, then spread the leaves over a large dish. Spoon the yoghurt dip into a small bowl and put it in the middle of the dish. Arrange the guinea fowl strips around it and serve.

TURKEY RAGOUT WITH COCONUT

1 Wash and pat dry the turkey breast fillet, then cut it into strips. Wash, halve, and de-seed the pepper, then cut it into strips.

2 Wash and trim the spring onions, and cut them into 5 cm pieces. Wash and pat dry the basil. Remove the stalks and finely chop half of the leaves. Set the other half aside for garnish.

3 Boil the coconut milk in the wok, stir in the turkey meat and curry paste, and simmer for about 1 minute. Stir occasionally. Add the prepared vegetables and simmer for another 3 minutes. Add the chopped basil, soy sauce, and sugar to taste.

SERVES 4

600 g turkey breast fillet
1 red pepper
250 g spring onions
1 bunch of basil
400 ml unsweetened coconut milk
1 tbsp red curry paste
2 tbsps soy sauce
1 tbsp sugar

PREPARATION TIME:
approx. 20 minutes
290 kcal/1221 kJ

113

TURKEY BREAST WITH LYCHEES

SERVES 4

4 turkey breasts*
3 shallots*
5 spring onions*
1 banana*
12 fresh lychees*
4 tbsps corn oil
1 tsp curry powder
Juice of 1 orange
100 ml creamed coconut
Salt
1 tsp cayenne pepper
2 tbsps freshly chopped coriander

PREPARATION TIME:
30 minutes
(plus cooking time)
approx. 355 kcal/1491 kJ

1 Cut the turkey meat in strips across the grain. Peel and slice the shallots into rings; wash and trim the spring onions, then cut them in half and chop them up. Peel and dice the banana. Peel the lychees and remove the stones.

2 Heat 2 tbsps oil in the wok and fry the meat all over until cooked. Remove the meat from the wok and set aside.

3 Heat the remaining oil in the wok and sweat the shallots and spring onions for about 1 minute. Stir in the curry, orange juice and coconut cream and bring the sauce to the boil.

4 Add the banana, lychees, turkey pieces and juices, and heat it all up, stirring constantly. Season to taste with salt and cayenne pepper. Serve sprinkled with coriander.

TIP

The asterisked ingredients can be replaced by an alternative. Use the spices and herbs according to taste. So you can use chicken or tofu instead of turkey breast, or just use more spring onions in place of shallots, or even everyday onions. Pineapple or mango can be substituted for lychees, and why not try a sharon fruit instead of the banana?

CHICKEN IN APRICOT SAUCE

1 Cut the chicken breast into pieces about 2 cm. Peel and finely chop the ginger, shallot, and garlic.

2 Mix half of the ginger with the chopped shallot and garlic, sesame oil and 3 tbsps soy sauce. Stir in the lemon grass, washed, trimmed and finely chopped.

3 Add the chicken and mix well. Cover and marinate in the fridge for at least 3 hours, and preferably overnight.

4 Mix the rest of the ginger with the sambal oelek, remaining soy sauce and lime juice. Wash, trim and cut the spring onions on the round, then mix them with the apricot jam.

5 Heat the oil in a wok and stir-fry the chicken. When the meat is just cooked, drizzle some of the marinade over it. Serve with the sauce.

SERVES 4

700 g chicken breast fillet

1 piece of fresh ginger (approx. 4 cm)

1 shallot

1 garlic clove

3 tbsps light sesame oil

6 tbsps light soy sauce

1 stem of lemon grass

½ tsp sambal oelek

2 tbsps lime juice

4 spring onions

4 tbsps apricot jam

2–3 tbsps oil for frying

PREPARATION TIME:
approx. 30 minutes
(plus marinating time)
245 kcal/1027 kJ

CHICKEN IN LEMON SAUCE

SERVES 4

700 g chicken breast fillet

1 egg yolk

2 tsps soy sauce

2 tbsps dry sherry

5 ½ tbsps cornflour

2 ½ tbsps wheat flour

Oil for deep-frying

80 ml lemon juice

2 tbsps sugar

4 spring onions, chopped into bite-size pieces, for garnish

PREPARATION TIME:

approx. 45 minutes

243 kcal/1021 kJ

1 Cut the chicken breast into 1 cm strips and put in a dish. Mix the egg yolk to a smooth paste in a bowl with 1 tbsp water, soy sauce, 1 tbsp sherry and 1 ½ tbsps cornflour. Pour the mixture over the meat, mix well, and leave to marinate for 10 minutes.

2 Sieve 3 tbsps of the cornflour and the flour onto a plate and dip the marinated chicken pieces in it. Heat oil in a wok and deep-fry the meat until golden brown.

Remove from the wok, drain on kitchen roll, then set aside.

3 Bring the lemon juice to the boil on a medium heat with 2 tbsps water, sugar, and the remaining sherry; stir until the sugar has dissolved. Mix the rest of the cornflour to a smooth paste with 1 tbsp water, then add slowly to the lemon sauce to thicken it, stirring all the time. Arrange the chicken on a serving dish and drizzle with the sauce.

LEMON DUCK

1 Boil the honey, aniseed liqueur, soy sauce, ginger, lemon zest and lemon juice for 10 minutes. Sieve and boil again until syrupy.

2 Season the duck legs with salt and pepper, then fry them slowly in oil for 12 minutes, skin-side down. Turn and fry for another 10 minutes. Brush regularly with the marinade as they are cooking.

3 Peel and halve the garlic cloves; wash and trim the leeks and cut them into 2 cm chunks on the diagonal. Fry the leeks in the butter for 10 minutes with the garlic and almonds. Serve with the duck legs and lemon syrup.

SERVES 4

3 tbsps honey

1 ½ tsps aniseed-based liqueur

1 tsp soy sauce

1 tsp ground ginger

Grated zest and juice of 1 unwaxed lemon

4 duck legs

Pepper, salt

1–2 tbsps olive oil

1 bulb of fresh garlic

2 leeks, 2 tbsps butter

1 tbsp shelled almonds

PREPARATION TIME:
approx. 15 minutes
(plus cooking time)
463 kcal/1943 kJ

DUCK ON LEMON GRASS SKEWERS

SERVES 4

200 g basmati rice
4 duck breasts
(each approx. 160 g)
10–12 lemon grass stems
5 garlic cloves
1 piece of fresh ginger
(approx. 3 cm)
225 ml hoisin sauce
225 ml soy sauce
4 tbsps sesame oil
5 cl rice wine
3–4 tbsps honey
1–2 tsps Chinese five-spice
powder
Salt
Pepper
125 g tempura flour
3 egg whites
2 small courgettes
Oil for deep-frying

PREPARATION TIME:
approx. 20 minutes
(plus cooking time)
610 kcal/2562 kJ

1 Cook the rice according to the packet instructions. Cut the duck breasts across the grain in 3–4 equal pieces.

2 Wash and trim the lemon grass, then use them to skewer the duck pieces.

3 Pre-heat the oven to 200 °C. Peel and crush the garlic. Peel and finely chop the ginger.

4 Make a marinade with the garlic, ginger, hoisin sauce, soy sauce, sesame oil, 4 cl rice wine, honey and Chinese five-spice powder.

5 Season the meat with salt and pepper, fry on the skin side until crispy, turn and fry for another 1 minute. Brush with the marinade.

6 Bake in the pre-heated oven for about 10 minutes. Brush with the marinade every couple of minutes.

7 Mix the tempura flour with a little water and the egg white.

8 Wash and trim the courgettes, then cut them into slices about 0.5 cm thick.

9 Heat the oil and dip the courgette slices in batter, adding them to the oil one at a time. Deep-fry until golden brown. Remove from the wok and drain on kitchen roll.

10 Boil the meat juices with the rest of the marinade and rice wine to make a smooth, thick sauce.

11 Strain the sauce and drizzle over the duck breast skewers, arranged on a dish with the courgettes.

GOOSE BREAST WITH CHICK PEAS

SERVES 4

300 g chick peas (tinned)
200 g alfalfa sprouts
1 bunch spring onions
100 g sweetcorn (tinned)
3–4 tbsps chilli oil
½ bunch savory
125 ml malt beer
Ground coriander, ground
cloves, and mustard powder
400 g smoked goose breast

PREPARATION TIME:
approx. 20 minutes
459 kcal/1930 kJ

1 Drain the chick peas well in a sieve. Wash and dry the alfalfa sprouts.

2 Wash and trim the spring onions, then cut them finely on the round. Drain the sweetcorn well in a sieve.

3 Heat the oil in the wok and stir-fry the vegetables in batches for 4–5 minutes.

4 Wash the savory, pat it dry, and pick off the leaves. Add it to the chick peas with the malt beer and cook on a medium heat for about 4–5 minutes.

5 Season the vegetables to taste with ground coriander and cloves and the mustard powder. Cut the goose breast into thin strips and serve with the chick pea mixture and alfalfa sprouts.

GOOSE BREAST WITH FRUIT

1 Cut the goose breast into strips. Wash and trim the leek, then cut into thin rings. Peel the pomelos and grapefruit, removing all the white pith. Then carefully fillet them into segments.

2 Cut the guavas into sections, then peel and dice them. Wash and peel the kaffir limes, then finely chop the peel. Wash the leaves and chop them finely as well. Wash, trim and finely chop the lemon grass.

3 Heat the oil in a wok and fry the meat for about 3 minutes. Then add the pomelos, grapefruit, leek, lime peel and leaves, guava and lemon grass. Season the mixture to taste with the spices. Cook for about 8 minutes, then serve in small bowls, garnished with lime slices.

SERVES 4

900 g smoked goose breast
1 leek
2 pomelos
2 pink grapefruit
2 guavas
4 kaffir limes
2 kaffir lime leaves
1 lemon grass stem
4 tbsps groundnut oil
1 tsp each of ground cardamom, aniseed, cloves, and ginger
Thin lime slices for garnish

PREPARATION TIME:
approx. 30 minutes
789 kcal/3315 kJ

DID YOU KNOW?

Pomelo is a large citrus fruit related to grapefruit varieties. It is pear-shaped, with a pale yellow to greenish skin.

123

CHICKEN WINGS WITH ORANGE SAUCE

1 Season the chicken wings with salt and pepper. Mix the sesame oil with the honey, carefully coat the chicken wings with it, and marinate for 30 minutes.

2 Heat the vegetable oil in a wok and sear the chicken wings on each side for 4 minutes until cooked.

3 Remove the wok from the heat, take the chicken wings out, and keep them warm. Wash the orange in hot water, rub it dry, remove the peel and grate off some zest. Squeeze juice from the orange.

4 Slowly heat the sugar without stirring until it caramelizes, then remove from the heat. Add the orange juice and browning juices. Stir over a low heat until you have a smooth sauce. If necessary, add a little water or orange juice.

5 Stir in half of the orange zest and simmer gently for 3 minutes. Arrange the chicken wings in a dish. Pour the orange sauce over the wings, sprinkle with the remaining zest and serve.

SERVES 4

12 chicken wings
Salt
Pepper
3 tbsps sesame oil
4–5 tbsps runny honey
5 tbsps vegetable oil
1 orange
1 ½ tbsps sugar

PREPARATION TIME:
approx. 40 minutes
(plus marinating time)
398 kcal/1670 kJ

CHICKEN IN GINGER WINE

SERVES 4

400 g chicken breast fillet
1 piece of fresh ginger (3 cm)
3 garlic cloves
3–4 tbsps sesame oil
Salt
Pepper
Ground ginger, ground coriander
3 tbsps spicy ketchup
4 cl dry sherry
2 cl plum brandy
½ bunch coriander leaves
Tabasco

PREPARATION TIME:
approx. 20 minutes
397 kcal/1668 kJ

1 Wash the chicken breast fillets, pat them dry, and cut into thin strips. Peel and finely grate the ginger. Peel and finely chop the garlic cloves.

2 Heat the oil in the wok and stir-fry the chicken strips with the ginger and garlic for about 5–6 minutes. Season with salt, pepper, ground ginger and ground coriander.

3 Add the ketchup, sherry and plum brandy to the wok and cook gently for another 3–5 minutes. Wash and dry the coriander, then pick off the leaves.

4 Add a final touch of Tabasco to the chicken and serve garnished with coriander. Goes well with prawn crackers.

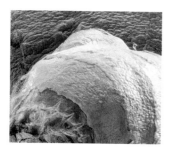  

TURKEY CURRY WITH CHILLI

SERVES 4

6 mild green jalapeño peppers

3 red chillies

1 yellow pepper

1 red pepper

1 turkey breast fillet

4 tbsps sesame oil

1 tbsp chilli oil

2 tbsps five-spice powder

3 tbsps green curry paste (ready-made)

750 ml chicken stock

3 tbsps fish sauce (ready-made)

3 tbsps light soy sauce

2 kaffir lime leaves

1 tbsp lemon juice

PREPARATION TIME:
approx. 35 minutes
571 kcal/2401 kJ

1 Wash all the peppers and chillies, cut them in half, remove the seeds and cut them into strips.

2 Wash the turkey fillet, pat dry, and cut into goujons. Heat up the oils and lightly braise the turkey meat.

3 Add the vegetables. Stir in the five-spice powder and curry paste. Then deglaze with the stock. Stir in the fish and soy sauces.

4 Wash, dry and finely chop the kaffir lime leaves, then add to the mixture along with the lemon juice. Simmer on a low heat for about 10 minutes. Serve with fragrant rice.

TIP

Alternatively, you can make your own green curry paste. For one jar, you will need: 3 shallots, 4 garlic cloves, 1 piece galangal, 6 green chillies, 1 stem lemon grass, 1 bunch coriander, 1 sprig mint, 1 unwaxed lime, 2 lime leaves, 1 tsp each of ground coriander, ground cumin, pepper, and salt, and 6 tbsps groundnut oil. Grind all the ingredients using a mortar and pestle, cover with a layer of oil in a jar and store in the refrigerator.

CHICKEN BREAST WITH TOFU

1 Wash and pat dry the chicken breast fillets, and cut them into thin strips. Peel and finely chop the shallots.

2 Rinse the pumpkin, baby corn and celeriac in a sieve and drain well. Cut it all into thin strips. Mix together the meat and vegetable strips.

3 Mix the oil with the hoisin sauce and rice wine, and pour it over the chicken and vegetable mix. Leave to marinate for about 15 minutes. Then braise it all in the wok for 8–10 minutes with the marinade.

4 Dice the tofu and fold it in carefully. Season liberally with five-spice powder and serve in small bowls.

SERVES 4

300 g chicken breast fillet

2 shallots

100 g pickled pumpkin

100 g baby corn (tinned)

100 g pickled celeriac

2–3 tbsps sesame oil

3–4 tbsps hoisin sauce (ready-made)

3–4 tbsps rice wine

100 g tofu

Five-spice powder

PREPARATION TIME:
approx. 30 minutes
(plus marinating and cooking time)
324 kcal/1363 kJ

 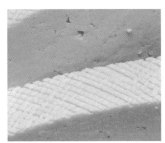 

SPICY CHICKEN LEGS

1 Wash and pat dry the chicken legs, then score across the skin. Trim and slice the mushrooms.

2 Wash, trim and slice the fennel. Keep the green leaves aside for garnish.

3 Nip off the ends of the mangetout and wash them. Peel and slice the parsnips.

4 Rub the spices well into the chicken legs and fry all over in the oil.

5 Put the vegetables in a bamboo steamer. Lay the chicken legs on top and steam it all together for 15–20 minutes over a rack in the wok.

6 Arrange the chicken legs and vegetables on a dish and serve garnished with fennel leaves.

SERVES 4

4 chicken legs
(each approx. 200 g)
200 g large flat mushrooms
100 g fennel
100 g mangetout
100 g parsnips
Salt
Pepper
Ground paprika
Mustard powder
2–3 tbsps groundnut or sesame oil

PREPARATION TIME:
approx. 30 minutes
625 kcal/2625 kJ

CRISPY DUCK WITH PINEAPPLE

SERVES 4

180–200 g wholemeal flour
1 tbsp walnut oil
4–5 tbsps milk
2–3 eggs
1 pinch salt
125 ml port
100 g desiccated coconut
2 baby pineapples
800 g duck breast fillet
Groundnut oil for deep-frying
150 g mandarins (tinned)
150 g sweet-sour pickled ginger
2–3 tbsps ketchup
Ground coriander, ground cloves and ground aniseed
Cayenne pepper
150 g mayonnaise
100 g natural yoghurt
1 small apple
1 banana
2 tbsps curry powder
1 tbsp chopped almonds
1 tbsp maple syrup
½ bunch lemon balm
1 unwaxed lemon

PREPARATION TIME:
approx. 30 minutes
1394 kcal/5869 kJ

1 Mix the flour to a smooth paste with the oil, milk, eggs, salt, port, and desiccated coconut. Peel the baby pineapples, quarter them, and remove the stalks.

2 Wash and pat dry the duck fillets and cut into pieces. Heat enough groundnut oil in the wok for deep-frying.

3 Dip the duck meat and pineapple quarters in the batter and deep-fry in batches for about 6–8 minutes. Remove them, drain on kitchen roll, and keep them warm.

4 For the red dip: drain the mandarins and ginger in a sieve. Season with ketchup, ground coriander, ground cloves, ground aniseed and cayenne pepper, and purée with a hand blender.

5 For the yellow dip: mix the mayonnaise and yoghurt to make a smooth paste. Peel and finely dice the apple and banana. Stir into the yoghurt mayonnaise with the curry powder, almonds, and maple syrup. Season to taste with salt.

6 Wash and dry the lemon balm, then pick off the leaves. Wash and slice the lemon.

7 Arrange the duck and pineapple pieces on a plate with the two dips. Serve garnished with lemon slices and lemon balm.

MEAT AND GAME

Whether it's hot and spicy or sweet-and-sour: meat lovers can expect a real treat thanks to the special way it is prepared in a wok. Frying the meat rapidly and at a high temperature makes it deliciously crispy on the outside and still tender and juicy on the inside. Discover all about Asian specialities using pork, beef, lamb and game, each blended harmoniously with the particular spices, herbs and vegetables which complement it.

SICHUAN-STYLE BEEF

1 Cut the beef into thin slices. Mix together the egg white, cornflour and 1 tbsp soy sauce, and marinate the beef in it.

2 Peel the onions and garlic, then cut the onions into thin rings. Wash, trim and finely chop the peppers and chillies. Wash, trim and cut the leek into thin strips. Wash, trim and dice the aubergine. Peel and finely chop the ginger.

3 Mix the sugar with the rest of the soy sauce, rice vinegar, and rice wine, and set aside.

4 Heat the oil in the wok. Fry the beef on a high heat, stirring continuously. Season with salt and pepper. Take the meat out of the wok and set to one side.

5 Heat a little oil, then brown the aubergines, onions, ginger and the rest of the vegetables, squeezing in the garlic. Stir-fry the mixture on a high heat. Mix in the meat. Pour in the sauce and mix all the ingredients thoroughly. Goes well with rice.

SERVES 4

500 g beef

1 egg white

1 tbsp cornflour

4 tbsps soy sauce

2 onions

2 garlic cloves

1 yellow and 1 green pepper

2 chillies

1 small leek

1 small aubergine

1 piece of fresh ginger (approx. 3 cm)

1 tsp sugar

1 tsp rice vinegar

2 tbsps rice wine

Oil for frying

A pinch of salt and pepper

PREPARATION TIME:
approx. 20 minutes
(plus cooking time)
278 kcal/1165 kJ

SPICY PEPPER STIR-FRY

SERVES 4

600 g rump steak
4–5 tbsps sesame oil
50 g green peppercorn in brine (jar)
100 g mandarins (tinned)
Salt
½ bunch spring onions

PREPARATION TIME:
approx. 20 minutes
449 kcal/1886 kJ

1 Cut the meat into thin strips. Heat the oil in the wok and stir-fry the meat strips for about 3–4 minutes.

2 Drain the peppercorns well, and add to the wok. Drain the mandarins well in a sieve, retaining the juice.

3 Add the mandarins to the wok and braise for about 1–2 minutes. Add 2–3 tbsps of the mandarin juice and a pinch of salt to taste.

4 Wash, dry and finely chop the spring onions on the round. Arrange the peppery stir-fry in a dish and sprinkle with chopped spring onions to serve.

DID YOU KNOW?

Rather confusingly, the name "pepper" is used for many hot berry or fruit spices: chillies in the form of "cayenne pepper", for example, or the ground leaves of the prickly-ash, which retail as "Sichuan" or "Sansho" pepper.

MASSAMAN BEEF CURRY

1 Slice the meat. Heat the oil in a wok. Add the curry paste and stir-fry well until the aromas are released.

2 Pour in the coconut milk, stirring all the time, and bring to the boil. Dice the potatoes, onions, peanuts, cinnamon, and cardamom and add to the wok. Cover and simmer for 20 minutes.

3 Add the meat mixture and let it soak in all the flavours for 10 minutes. Season with the fish sauce, tamarind juice and palm sugar. Serve as soon as the potatoes and meat are fully cooked.

SERVES 4

500 g fillet of beef

2 tbsps oil

4 tbsps Massaman curry paste

1 litre coconut milk

500 g diced potatoes

1 chopped onion

75 g unsalted peanuts

1 cinnamon stick

A few cardamom seeds

3 tbsps fish sauce

3 tbsps tamarind juice

2 tbsps palm sugar

PREPARATION TIME:
approx. 15 minutes
(plus cooking time)
335 kcal/1407 kJ

TANGY LAMB STRIPS

SERVES 4

500 g lamb fillet
2–3 tbsps sesame oil
Salt
Pepper
Ground ginger, ground cardamom, garlic powder
1 pinch dried rosemary
250 g mixed pickles
1–2 tbsps sour cream

PREPARATION TIME:
approx. 40 minutes
267 kcal/1121 kJ

1 Wash and pat dry the meat, then cut it into thin strips. Mix the oil and spices, and marinate the meat strips in it for about 15–20 minutes.

2 Put the meat into a heated wok along with the marinade and stir-fry for about 5–6 minutes.

3 Add the mixed pickles with their liquid and braise for 3–4 minutes. Stir in the sour cream, arrange the meat strips and vegetables in small bowls and serve.

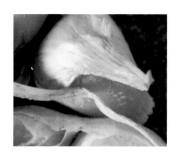

SPICY PORK STIR-FRY

SERVES 4

1 kg lean pork fillet

12 garlic cloves

2 shallots

1 ½ tsps freshly ground black pepper

3 tbsps fish sauce (ready-made)

2 tbsps red wine vinegar

1 tbsp light soy sauce

1 tbsp dark soy sauce

1 tbsp yellow curry paste (ready-made)

1 tbsp chilli sauce (ready-made)

1 bitter melon

100 g black olives, stones removed

5 tbsps sunflower oil

2 tbsps sesame seeds

Freshly grated nutmeg

PREPARATION TIME:
approx. 40 minutes
(plus marinating time)
634 kcal/2665 kJ

1 Cut the meat into 4 × 2 cm strips and put them in a bowl.

2 Peel and finely slice the garlic. Peel and dice the shallots.

3 Mix the garlic and shallots with the pepper, fish sauce, red wine vinegar, soy sauce, curry paste and chilli sauce.

4 Pour the sauce over the meat, cover and marinate for about 1 hour.

5 Wash the bitter melon, cut it lengthways and then into slices. Drain the olives and cut them in half.

6 Heat the oil in a wok and brown the meat. Add the bitter melon, olives and sesame seeds.

7 Season with nutmeg and simmer for another 7 minutes. Arrange on plates and serve.

HOT PORK CURRY

1 Cut the meat into small cubes. Heat the oil in the wok and sear the meat, stirring all the time. Scoop the meat out and keep it warm.

2 Peel and finely chop the onion and garlic. Add along with the vegetable stock, plum sauce and curry paste to the oil still in the wok, and simmer on a gentle heat for about 2–3 minutes.

3 Add the meat and simmer for another 6–7 minutes. Sprinkle roasted pine nut kernels over the curry and serve with rice.

SERVES 4

600 g boneless pork chops

5–6 tbsps sesame oil

1 onion

1 garlic clove

125 ml vegetable stock

1 tbsp plum sauce
(ready-made)

2 tbsps green curry paste

1–2 tbsps pine nut kernels

PREPARATION TIME:
approx. 20 minutes
360 kcal/1513 kJ

VENISON WITH PLUMS

SERVES 4

400 g venison fillet

4–5 tbsps sesame oil

150 g plums (jar)

125 ml venison or beef stock (ready-made)

3–4 tbsps plum jelly

3–4 tbsps dark beer

1 tbsp red wine vinegar

Salt

Cayenne pepper

Ground ginger, ground cloves and ground coriander

½ bunch coriander leaves

PREPARATION TIME:
approx. 20 minutes
295 kcal/1241 kJ

1 Cut the meat into thin strips. Heat the oil in the wok and stir-fry the meat for about 3–4 minutes.

2 Drain the plums well in a sieve. Add to the meat and deglaze with the stock.

3 Add the plum jelly, dark beer and vinegar, then simmer for about 6–8 minutes. Season well with salt, cayenne pepper, ground ginger, cloves and coriander.

4 Wash, dry and finely chop the coriander leaves. Arrange the meat in a serving dish and serve sprinkled with coriander leaves.

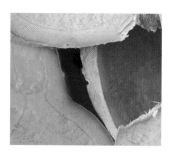

RABBIT FILLET WITH GRAPES

SERVES 4

300 g green grapes
50 g raisins
4 cl Armagnac (or Cognac)
½ tbsp five-spice powder
500 g rabbit fillet
2–3 tbsps sesame oil
100 g diced bacon
Salt
Pepper
100 g lentil sprouts

PREPARATION TIME:
approx. 30 minutes
347 kcal/1459 kJ

1 Wash, halve and de-stone the grapes. Mix the grapes with the raisins, Armagnac and five-spice powder, and leave to marinate for about 10–15 minutes.

2 Cut the rabbit fillet into thin strips. Heat the oil in the wok and stir-fry the meat strips and diced bacon for about 3–4 minutes.

3 Add the grape mixture and simmer for about 3–4 minutes. Season well with salt and pepper. Wash the lentil sprouts, drain well, and add to the wok. Heat up for a couple of minutes, arrange in a dish, and serve.

STUFFED MEAT ROLLS

1 Finely chop the ham, onion and garlic, then mix in the star anise and cinnamon.

2 Wipe and trim the mushrooms, then chop them finely. Crumble the feta and mix with the sesame oil, mushrooms and chopped ham. Season with salt and pepper.

3 Cut the escalopes in half lengthways. Spread on a work surface and brush thinly with horseradish.

4 Spread the meat mixture on each escalope and roll them up. Hold in place with wooden cocktail sticks.

5 Heat the oil in the wok and sear the rolls of meat, turning them round. Remove the rolls and wipe down the wok.

6 Add the chicken stock to the wok and heat it up. Place the meat rolls in a bamboo steamer. Put the steamer onto a rack in the wok, cover and steam the meat rolls for about 15–20 minutes over the stock. Arrange the meat rolls on a plate and serve with a side dish of hoisin sauce.

SERVES 4

100 g cooked ham

1 onion

1 garlic clove

½ tsp each of star anise and cinnamon

100 g shiitake mushrooms

100 g feta cheese

2–3 tbsps sesame oil

Salt, pepper

400 g very thin veal or pork escalopes

2–3 tbsps creamed horseradish

4–5 tbsps groundnut oil

250–500 ml chicken stock (ready-made or cube)

Hoisin sauce (ready-made) as an accompaniment

PREPARATION TIME:
approx. 40 minutes
508 kcal/2136 kJ

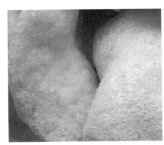

STEAMED SAVOY PARCELS

SERVES 4

8–10 medium-size savoy
cabbage leaves
Salt
1 bunch parsley
1 tbsp capers
1 small onion
1 garlic clove
1 egg
1–2 tbsps oregano leaves
1 tsp caraway seeds
400 g ground pork
Cayenne pepper

PREPARATION TIME:
approx. 30 minutes
376 kcal/1581 kJ

1 Wash the cabbage leaves and blanch them in boiling salted water for 1–2 minutes. Remove from pan, plunge briefly in cold water, and dry them.

2 Wash, dry and finely chop the parsley. Finely chop the capers, onion and garlic as well. Knead the parsley, capers, egg, oregano, caraway seeds, onion, garlic and ground pork into a smooth meat paste. Season with salt and pepper and divide the mixture between the savoy leaves.

3 Fold in the sides of the leaves and roll them up. Hold the parcels in place with cocktail sticks. Bring salted water to the boil in the wok and place the cabbage parcels in a bamboo steamer.

4 Put the steamer onto a rack in the wok, cover and steam for about 10–15 minutes. Then carefully lift out the cabbage parcels, arrange on a plate and serve.

STEAMED CHARD

SERVES 4

20 large chard leaves
2 stems of lemon grass
1 garlic clove
1 bread roll
100 g galangal root
500 g pork mince
3 eggs
1 tbsp hoisin sauce
1 tsp finely grated ginger
Some coriander oil

PREPARATION TIME:
approx. 50 minutes
376 kcal/1576 kJ

1 Wash the chard leaves and blanch them briefly. Cut one of the lemon grass stalks into sections, and finely chop one of them along with the peeled garlic clove. Soak the bread roll, then peel and chop the galangal.

2 Mix together the pork mince, eggs, squeezed-out bread roll, finely chopped lemon grass and garlic, the hoisin sauce, and ginger.

3 Divide the filling between the blanched chard leaves and form them into rounds. Line bamboo steamers with galangal root and lemon grass pieces, place the chard rounds on top, and drizzle with coriander oil.

4 Heat water in the wok, place the bamboo steamers on a rack over the water, cover, and steam for about 30 minutes.

PORK FILLET WITH LIME

1 Cut the pork into 2 cm pieces. Marinate for 10 minutes in the fish and oyster sauces. Slice the limes. Wash and shake the coriander dry, then pick off the leaves.

2 Line four bamboo steamers with the lime slices, lay the marinated meat on top, and sprinkle with coriander leaves. Put the lids on the steamers.

3 Heat some water in the wok, and place the steamers on a rack over the water. Swap the top and bottom steamers round after 5 minutes to ensure even cooking.

4 Leave the steamed meat uncovered for 6–8 minutes, then serve sprinkled with pink peppercorns.

SERVES 4

600 g pork fillet
4 tbsps fish sauce
4 tbsps oyster sauce
4 limes
1 bunch coriander
4 tsps pink peppercorns

PREPARATION TIME:
approx. 25 minutes
(plus marinating time)
205 kcal/858 kJ

LAMB BIRYANI

SERVES 4

1 tsp saffron threads
250 g basmati rice
2 garlic cloves
2 onions
1 piece of fresh ginger
(approx. 2 cm)
600 g lamb
Salt, 2 cloves
½ tsp black peppercorns
2 green cardamom pods
1 tsp cumin
2 cm piece of cinnamon
stick
2 tbsps ghee or clarified
butter
Nutmeg, chilli powder
180 g natural yoghurt
4 tbsps raisins, 4 tbsps
flaked almonds

PREPARATION TIME:
approx. 40 minutes
(plus cooking time)
580 kcal/2436 kJ

1 Soak the saffron in lukewarm water and set aside. Wash the basmati rice, then soak it in cold water for 30 minutes.

2 Peel the garlic and onions, then slice the onions. Peel and grate the ginger. Cut the lamb into bite-size pieces.

3 Boil a pan of salted water, bring the rice briefly to the boil, then simmer on a very low heat for 15 minutes. Finely grind the garlic, ginger, cloves, pepper, cardamom, cumin and cinnamon with a pestle and mortar.

4 Fry the onions in the wok until golden brown. Add the spice mix and some freshly ground nutmeg and chilli powder, then stir-fry for 1 minute. Add the lamb and brown evenly all over.

5 Stir in the yoghurt and the ghee with the raisins and saffron water, bring to the boil, and cook for 40 minutes. Dry-roast the almonds in a pan.

6 Make a rice pyramid on a plate, sprinkle with the toasted almonds, arrange the meat around the rice, and serve.

LAMB WITH GREEN PEPPER

SERVES 4

500 g boned leg of lamb

2 each of yellow, green and red peppers

10 large Mexican pepperleaves

4 tbsps vegetable oil

1 tsp curry powder

1 tsp five-spice powder

2 tbsps ground green peppercorns

PREPARATION TIME:
approx. 25 minutes
435 kcal/1822 kJ

1 Cut the lamb into small cubes. Wash, dry and de-seed the peppers, then cut them into diamond-shaped pieces. Cut two of the pepperleaves into very fine strips.

2 Heat the oil in the wok, sear the lamb cubes briefly in it. Dust with the curry and five-spice powder and remove from the wok.

3 Sear the peppers all over in the wok, then deglaze with 200 ml water. Add the peppercorns and reduce the liquid almost completely.

4 Return the lamb to the wok and mix in the pepperleaf strips. Line each plate with 2 pepperleaves and arrange the meat on top.

TIP

The leaves of the Mexican Hoja Santa pepper plant can be obtained fresh or dried in good delicatessens. They have an aromatic flavour reminiscent of aniseed, nutmeg and pepper.

LAMB SHOULDER WITH CUMIN

1 Cut the lamb into thin slices. Mix with the curry, ground cumin and ground coriander seeds.

2 Peel and finely slice the shallots, peel and finely chop the garlic. Wash and trim the spinach, then shake it dry.

3 Heat the oil in the wok, then quickly sear the shallots, garlic and chilli flakes. Add the meat and hoisin sauce, and sauté.

4 Next add the spinach and cook briefly until wilted. Deglaze with a little water, stir carefully, and serve.

SERVES 4

500 g shoulder or saddle of lamb

1 tsp curry powder

1 tsp ground cumin

1 tsp coriander seeds

3 shallots

2 garlic cloves

400 g fresh leaf spinach

4 tbsps vegetable oil

½ tsp chilli flakes

1 tsp hoisin sauce

PREPARATION TIME:
approx. 25 minutes
594 kcal/2487 kJ

BEEF WITH SPINACH AND MANGO

1 Cut the meat into strips. Rinse the spinach thoroughly under running water, shake it dry, and chop it roughly.

2 Peel the mango and cut the flesh into diamond shapes. Wash and chop the chillies.

3 Heat the oil in the wok and sauté the spinach and chillies briefly in it, then remove them from the wok.

4 Sear the meat strips in the same oil. Deglaze with soy sauce and stir well.

5 Next add the mango pieces. Then put the spinach and chillies back in the wok and mix through the meat.

6 Season with sweet-and-sour sauce, and serve sprinkled with Thai basil leaves.

SERVES 4

500 g beef
200 g leaf spinach
1 ripe mango
2 mild green chillies
3 tbsps vegetable oil
2 tbsps soy sauce
3 tbsps sweet-and-sour sauce
½ bunch Thai basil

PREPARATION TIME:
approx. 30 minutes
460 kcal/1925 kJ

CHOP SUEY

SERVES 4

12 dried morel mushrooms

500 g pork

Salt

2 tbsps soy sauce

2 tsps cornflour

1 onion

200 g bamboo shoots
(jar or tin)

200 g bean sprouts
(jar or tin)

1 red pepper

1 leek

Oil for frying

3 tbsps rice wine

Black pepper

1 tsp sugar

PREPARATION TIME:

approx. 45 minutes
(plus soaking time)
373 kcal/1565 kJ

1 Soak the dried morel mushrooms for at least 30 minutes in hot water. Dice the pork and mix with a pinch of salt, 1 tbsp soy sauce and the cornflour.

2 Peel and roughly chop the onion. Drain the bamboo shoots and cut them into strips. Drain the bean sprouts.

3 Wash the pepper, cut it in half and remove the stalk and seeds, then chop it into small pieces. Rinse the mushrooms well and drain. Wash, trim and slice the leek.

4 Heat the oil in the wok, sweat the onions, and then brown the meat. Add the rest of the soy sauce and rice wine, and simmer for 4 minutes. Take the mixture out of the wok and keep it warm.

5 Re-heat the oil and stir-fry the bean sprouts, peppers, leek, bamboo shoots and mushrooms for 3–4 minutes. Season with pepper and sugar. Arrange the vegetables and meat on a dish and serve.

SHREDDED PORK WITH CHARD

SERVES 4

400 g pork escalope
Some flour
Salt
Pepper
3–4 tbsps groundnut oil
1 tbsp chilli oil
500 g chard
3 shallots
125 ml veal or chicken stock
(ready-made or cube)
100 g Parma ham
50 g slivered almonds

PREPARATION TIME:
approx. 30 minutes
369 kcal/1550 kJ

1 Cut the escalopes into strips. Dip in flour seasoned with salt and pepper. Heat the two oils in the wok and stir-fry the meat strips for about 4–5 minutes. Remove the meat from the wok and keep it warm.

2 Wash, dry and finely chop the chard. Peel and finely chop the shallots. Fry the shallots and chard in the remaining oil for 2–3 minutes.

3 Deglaze with the stock and simmer gently for 4–5 minutes. Cut the Parma ham into thin strips and add to the mixture along with the pork strips.

4 Dry-roast the slivered almonds in a pan. Arrange the shredded meat on a plate and serve sprinkled with the almonds.

BEEF FILLET WITH SPRING ONIONS

1 Cut the meat into strips. Mix the cornflour with the egg white and vegetable oil, and soak the meat in it for about 20 minutes.

2 Wash and trim the spring onions, cut them into 4 cm lengths, and press them flat with a knife. Mix together the sherry, soy sauce and salt.

3 Heat the groundnut oil in the wok or a large pan. Remove the meat strips from the marinade and put them in a heatproof sieve in small batches. Dip each batch in the hot fat briefly and take it out again. Repeat this process, re-heating the oil each time. Then drain the meat and pour off most of the oil from the pan or wok, leaving 1 tbsp.

4 Sweat the spring onions in this oil for about 1 minute. Add the soy sauce mixture and the meat, and simmer for another minute, stirring all the time. Drizzle with sesame oil and serve.

SERVES 4

400 g beef fillet
3 tsps cornflour
1 egg white
3 tbsps vegetable oil
16 spring onions
1 tbsp sherry
1 tbsp dark soy sauce
1 tbsp light soy sauce
¼ tsp salt
Groundnut oil for deep frying
1 tbsp sesame oil

PREPARATION TIME:
30 minutes (plus marinating time)
approx. 247 kcal/1038 kJ

STEWED PORK

SERVES 4

650 g pork shoulder
3–4 tbsps sesame oil
3 tbsps sherry vinegar
6 tbsps soy sauce
4 tbsps honey
1 tbsp five-spice powder
125–250 ml veal or chicken stock (ready-made)
100 g mixed vegetables for soup (available frozen)
100 g pickled pearl onions
1 tsp cornflour
Mango chutney (jar) for serving

PREPARATION TIME:
approx. 35 minutes (plus cooking time)
674 kcal/2830 kJ

1 Cut the meat into small pieces. Heat the oil in the wok and sear the meat for 4–5 minutes.

2 Mix together the vinegar, soy sauce, honey, five-spice powder, and stock. Add to the meat along with the mixed vegetables and pearl onions, and simmer for 15–20 minutes, stirring occasionally.

3 Add a little more soy sauce at this stage if you like. Remove the meat and keep it warm.

4 Mix the cornflour to a smooth paste with some cold water and thicken the stock with it.

5 Arrange the meat and vegetables in a dish and serve with mango chutney.

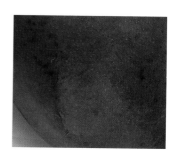

ASIAN GOULASH

1 Cut the meat into small, even pieces. Peel and finely chop the onion and garlic.

2 Sauté the onions, garlic and mixed vegetables in the groundnut oil for 2–3 minutes. Add the meat and stir-fry for about 3–4 minutes.

3 Drain the lentils well in a sieve. Add to the meat in the wok along with the chicken stock and simmer gently for about 4–5 minutes.

4 Season with soy sauce, vinegar and spices to make a spicy goulash.

5 Wash, pat dry and finely chop the coriander leaves. Arrange the goulash in a dish and serve sprinkled with the chopped coriander.

SERVES 4

600 g pork fillet

2–3 red onions

2 garlic cloves

100 g mixed vegetables for soup (available frozen)

4–5 tbsps groundnut oil

300–400 g lentils (pre-packed)

125 ml chicken stock (ready-made or cube)

1–2 tbsps soy sauce

1–2 tbsps apple vinegar

Salt

Pepper

Ground cloves

1 pinch sugar

½ bunch coriander

PREPARATION TIME:
approx. 20 minutes
589 kcal/2474 kJ

MONGOLIAN LAMB FILLET

SERVES 4

1 kg fillet of lamb
3 garlic cloves
1 piece of fresh ginger
(approx. 2 cm)
4 large onions
1 tbsp hoisin sauce
1 tbsp sesame oil
2 tbsps sesame seeds
2 tbsps groundnut oil
½ bunch spring onions
3 tsps cornflour
3 tbsps soy sauce
75 cl rice wine

PREPARATION TIME:
approx. 40 minutes (plus
marinating time)
438 kcal/1838 kJ

1 Cut the lamb across the grain in slices. Peel the garlic, ginger and onions.

2 Cut the onions into quarters and finely chop the garlic and ginger. Mix with the hoisin sauce and sesame oil. Turn the meat around in this marinade, cover, and leave in fridge for 1 hour.

3 Dry-roast the sesame seeds on a medium heat for 3 minutes until golden, stirring continuously. Then remove from pan to stop them from becoming burnt.

4 Heat the groundnut oil in a wok and stir-fry the quartered onions on a medium heat for 10 minutes until golden. Spoon the onions out of the wok and keep warm.

5 Heat the wok up again and sear the meat in batches over a high heat. Then put all of the meat back in the wok.

6 Chop the spring onions on the round. Mix the cornflour to a smooth paste with the soy sauce and rice wine, and stir into the meat. Continue to stir-fry the meat over a high heat until it is cooked and the sauce thickens.

7 Spoon the meat on top of the onions and serve sprinkled with toasted sesame seeds and spring onions.

SWEET-SOUR VENISON

1 Cut the diced meat into smaller pieces if necessary. Mix together the vinegar, red wine, mustard, oil and spices. Pour over the meat and leave to marinate for about 10–15 minutes.

2 Heat the wok and stir-fry the meat with the marinade for about 10–15 minutes.

3 Drain the beetroot well in a sieve, then cut into fine strips. Peel the onions and cut into rings.

4 Add the beetroot and onions to the goulash 5 minutes before the end of cooking time. Serve the goulash on a bed of wild rice.

SERVES 4

600 g diced venison

3–4 tbsps raspberry vinegar

4–5 tbsps red wine

1 tsp hot Chinese mustard

5–6 tbsps sesame oil

Salt

Pepper

Ground cloves, ground aniseed and ground cardamom

300 g pickled beetroot (jar)

200 g red onions

PREPARATION TIME:

approx. 40 minutes (plus marinating time)
350 kcal/1473 kJ

SPICY STUFFED ROTI

SERVES 4

375 g atta or wheat flour
Salt
3 tbsps ghee
2 eggs
Oil
2 chopped shallots
3 garlic cloves
2 tsps ground cumin
1 tsp ground turmeric
500 g lean beef or lamb mince
3 red chillies, finely chopped
Oil or ghee for frying

PREPARATION TIME:
approx. 50 minutes
(plus resting time)
603 kcal/2530 kJ

1 Mix the flour and 1 tsp salt. Rub in 2 tbsps ghee. Add an egg, beaten with 250 ml water, and mix it all into a moist dough.

2 Put the dough on a floured work surface and knead for 10 minutes. Brush with oil, wrap in cling-film, and leave to rest for at least 2 hours.

3 Heat the rest of the ghee. Sweat the shallots for 5 minutes.

4 Peel the garlic and squeeze it into the ghee along with the cumin and turmeric, then sweat for another 1 minute.

5 Add the mince and stir-fry. Mix in the chillies and season with salt.

6 Divide the dough into 12 portions and roll them into balls. Using lightly oiled fingertips, pull the dough balls gently out from the edges into rounds measuring about 15 cm. Cover with cling-film.

7 Beat 1 egg. Rub the wok with oil and carefully place one of the dough rounds (roti) in it. Brush with egg, put 2 heaped tbsps of filling on it and fry until the underside of the roti is golden brown.

8 Fold over the roti, press the edges together, and keep it warm.

9 Fry the remaining roti using the same process. Keep the cooked roti warm in the oven.

SWEET-AND-SOUR PORK

1 Cut the meat into thin strips. Mix the cornflour in a bowl along with the soy sauce, vinegar, rice wine, horseradish, and kecap manis. Stir in the cayenne pepper, and marinate the meat for 15 minutes in the mixture.

2 Dice the pineapple, wash and trim the leek and cut on the round. Wash, trim, de-seed and dice the pepper. De-seed and finely chop the chilli.

3 Heat 2 tbsps oil in a wok. In turn, fry the leek, pepper and chilli for about 5 minutes. Heat the remaining oil in another pan. Take the meat out of the marinade and pat it dry. Brown well in the hot oil.

4 Stir the meat into the vegetable mixture along with the pineapple and marinade. Season with salt and pepper. Serve with rice.

SERVES 4

600 g pork fillet

1 tsp cornflour

2 tbsps soy sauce

1 tbsp sherry vinegar

6 tbsps rice wine

1 tsp freshly grated horseradish

1 tbsp kecap manis (Indonesian sweet soy sauce)

¼ tsp cayenne pepper

½ pineapple, peeled

1 leek

1 green pepper

1 red chilli

3 tbsps groundnut oil

Salt and pepper

PREPARATION TIME:

35 minutes
(plus marinating time)
approx. 207 kcal/869 kJ

FISH

Countries in Asia are surrounded by the sea, so fish dishes have traditionally played a major role in their cuisine. Whether it's deep-fried, braised or steamed, in the form of fish balls, fillets or curry, wok cooking has a widely diverse range of recipes for fans of easy fish-based meals.

FISH IN BANANA LEAVES

1 Cut the fish into 5 × 2 cm pieces. Soak the chillies in warm water. Blend the coriander, desiccated coconut, spring onions, garlic, ginger, lemon grass, chillies (drained and dried), cashew nuts, and groundnut oil. Sweat the paste in a wok for 3 minutes. Add the coconut milk, reduce it and season with salt and pepper.

2 Steam the banana leaves for 1 minute in boiling water. Pat them dry and brush one side with oil. Pre-heat the grill to 180 °C.

3 Put a spoonful of paste on a banana leaf, lay a piece of fish on it, and brush the top with paste. Wrap up the banana leaf. Grill the fish parcel on each side for about 8 minutes, and serve hot. Open the parcel at the table.

MAKES 15 PORTIONS

250 g fish fillet, e.g. red snapper

2 dried red chillies

½ tbsp roasted coriander seeds

50 g desiccated coconut

2 spring onions

1 garlic clove

1 tsp freshly grated ginger

½ stem of lemon grass

10 cashew nuts

1 tbsp groundnut oil

90 ml thin coconut milk

Salt, pepper

15 banana leaves

Vegetable oil

PREPARATION TIME:
30 minutes
(plus cooking time)
Each piece approx.
220 kcal/925 kJ

STEAMED CARP

SERVES 4

1–1 ½ kg carp fillet

2–3 tbsps rice wine or dry sherry

2–3 tbsps coarse sea salt

2–3 tbsps coarsely ground pepper

4 shallots

1 piece of fresh ginger (3 cm)

2 red peppers

100 g bamboo shoots (tinned)

5–6 tbsps soy sauce

500 ml fish stock (ready-made)

2–3 tbsps Chinese mustard

1 tbsp cornflour

2–3 tbsps sour cream

PREPARATION TIME:
approx. 40 minutes
409 kcal/1720 kJ

1 Wash the fish fillets and pat them dry, then drizzle with the rice wine. Rub in salt and pepper and place them in a steamer.

2 Peel and quarter the shallots. Peel and slice the ginger. Halve, de-seed and wash the peppers, then cut them into diamond shapes.

3 Put the bamboo shoots in a sieve and drain well. Mix all the vegetables and drizzle with the soy sauce.

4 Spread the vegetable mix over the fish. Bring the fish stock to the boil in the wok. Place the steamer over the rack in the wok and steam gently for about 15–20 minutes.

5 Remove the steamer and stir the mustard into about 350 ml of fish stock. Mix the cornflour with a little cold water and thicken the fish stock with it. Season the sauce to taste and finish it off with the sour cream.

6 Arrange the carp pieces on plates with the vegetables and sauce, and serve.

SEA BASS ROLLS

1 Wash, trim and finely dice the courgette and leeks. Remove the skins and seeds of the tomatoes, then dice the flesh. Peel and chop the carrots. Wash the mushrooms and cut them into small pieces.

2 Cut the ham into thin strips. Season the vegetables with the five-spice powder. Heat the oil in the wok and stir-fry the vegetables and ham for 4–5 minutes.

3 Wash the fish fillets, pat them dry, and cut them into thin strips on the diagonal. Spread a very thin layer of wasabi on them and then a layer of the vegetable and ham mixture. Roll them up and hold them in place with cocktail sticks.

4 Heat the fish stock and soy sauce in the wok. Put the fish rolls in a bamboo steamer. Place the steamer on a rack over the liquid in the wok, and gently cook the fish for about 4–5 minutes. Serve the fish rolls with basmati rice.

SERVES 4

1 courgette

2 thin leeks

3 tomatoes

3 carrots

200 g large, flat mushrooms

100 g cooked ham

1 tbsp five-spice powder

3–4 tbsps sesame oil

4 sea bass fillets (each 200 g)

1–2 tbsps wasabi

500–750 ml fish stock (ready-made or cube)

2–3 tbsps soy sauce

PREPARATION TIME:
approx. 35 minutes
328 kcal/1379 kJ

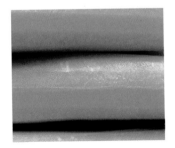

BRAISED EEL WITH FENNEL

SERVES 4

800 g eel
4–5 tbsps sherry vinegar
1 tbsp coarse sea salt
50 g pickled ginger
200 g parsnips
300 g fennel
6–7 tbsps sesame oil
1 tbsp fennel seeds
Salt
Cayenne pepper
125–250 ml fish stock
(ready-made)
½ bunch parsley
Strips of lemon peel for
garnish

PREPARATION TIME:
approx. 35 minutes
(plus marinating time)
293 kcal/1232 kJ

1 Wash the eel and cut it into 3–4 cm pieces. Drizzle with the vinegar and sprinkle on the sea salt. Leave to soak for about 5–8 minutes.

2 Drain the ginger well in a sieve. Wash, trim and chop the parsnips and fennel.

3 Heat the oil in the wok and stir-fry the eel for 4–5 minutes.

4 Add the ginger, parsnip, fennel, and fennel seeds and fry for another 3–4 minutes. Season with salt and cayenne pepper and pour in the stock. Braise gently for about 6–8 minutes.

5 Wash, dry and pick the leaves off the parsley. Arrange the braised eel on a dish with parsley and lemon strips and serve.

TIP

Eel isn't everyone's cup of tea. If this applies to you, try using salmon fillets instead, in which case you do not need to fry it separately.

SWEET-AND-SOUR FISH WITH ONIONS

1 Peel and dice the shallots. Heat the groundnut oil in the wok and fry the shallots for 5–6 minutes.

2 Add the vinegar, fish stock, bay leaf, spices, chillies, thyme, salt and sugar and simmer gently for 6–8 minutes.

3 Wash and pat dry the fish fillet, then chop it into small pieces. Coat the fish pieces in cornflour.

4 Add the fish to the onion mixture. Stir-fry on a low heat for about 5–6 minutes.

5 Arrange the fish and onions on a dish with the sauce and serve. Goes well with rice.

SERVES 4

500 g shallots

5–6 tbsps groundnut oil

6 tbsps sherry vinegar

250 ml fish stock (ready-made or cube)

1 crushed bay leaf

Ground cloves, ground ginger, mustard powder

Coarsely ground black pepper

1–2 dried crushed chillies

1 tsp thyme leaves

Salt

Sugar

500 g white fish fillet

2 tsps cornflour

PREPARATION TIME:
approx. 25 minutes
342 kcal/1438 kJ

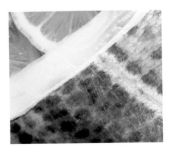

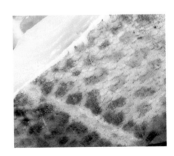

FISH CURRY WITH BAMBOO SHOOTS

1 Wash, trim and finely chop the spring onions. Wash and trim the bamboo shoots, and cut them into 5 cm pieces. Sweat in a little oil in the wok until they are almost tender.

2 Wash the kaffir lime leaves and Thai basil leaves, then cut them into thin strips. Set to one side. Wash, trim and halve the chillies, removing the stalk and seeds, then chop them finely.

3 Peel and de-vein the prawns. Cut the fish into pieces. Fry the fish pieces, prawns and spring onions in the wok in groundnut oil. Remove from wok and keep warm.

4 Bring the coconut cream to the boil in the wok, simmer, stirring continuously until the surface has a glossy sheen. Mix in the curry paste, coconut milk and bamboo shoots, then add the fish sauce, sugar, kaffir lime leaves and chillies.

5 Bring it all to the boil, fold in the fish and prawns and heat them up. Season the fish curry to taste, and serve garnished with Thai basil.

SERVES 4

1 bunch spring onions
200 g fresh bamboo shoots
Groundnut oil for frying
4 kaffir lime leaves
1 bunch Thai basil leaves
2 fresh red chillies
8 king prawns
600 g monkfish fillet
Approx. 225 ml coconut cream
1 ½ tsps red curry paste
500 ml coconut milk
2 tbsps fish sauce
2 tsps sugar

PREPARATION TIME:
approx. 10 minutes
(plus cooking time)
158 kcal/664 kJ

DEEP-FRIED FISH SLICES

SERVES 4

500 g fish fillet
(fresh or frozen)
1 small onion
1 garlic clove
1 sachet Provençal herbs
100 g bacon bits
Salt and pepper
Ground ginger and mustard
powder
2–3 eggs
1 medium-size baguette
50–100 g sesame seeds
Groundnut oil for
deep-frying
1 lemon
Plum sauce (ready-made)

PREPARATION TIME:
approx. 35 minutes
514 kcal/2160 kJ

1 Defrost the fish fillet and mince finely along with the onion, garlic and Provençal herbs. Mix in the bacon bits.

2 Season the fish filling with salt, pepper, ground ginger and mustard powder. Beat the eggs. Cut the bread into thin slices and make some notches along the crusts.

3 Brush the bread slices with a little beaten egg. Divide the fish mixture between the slices and sprinkle with sesame seeds. Press them down well and brush with some more egg.

4 Heat the oil in the wok. Place the bread slices, with the filling side down, on the slotted ladle and dip them into the oil. Deep-fry them gently for 3–4 minutes until crispy.

5 Drain the fish slices on kitchen roll. Cut the lemon into 8 wedges. Serve the fish garnished with lemon wedges and the plum sauce on the side.

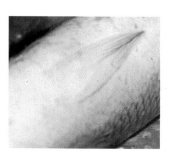

CRISPY FISH WITH SESAME CRUST

1 Wash and dry the fish fillet and partly freeze in the freezer. Take it out and cut it into thin slices.

2 Mix together the salt, pepper, oil and rice wine. Wash and trim the spring onions, then cut them on the round. Peel and finely chop the ginger.

3 Add the spring onions and ginger to the marinade and pour over the fish slices. Leave to marinate for about 10–15 minutes.

4 Put the flour on a flat plate. Beat the eggs and have the sesame seeds ready in a dish.

5 Heat some groundnut oil in a wok, enough for deep-frying. Remove the fish slices from the marinade and dip in turn in the flour, egg and sesame seeds.

6 Deep-fry the fish pieces in the hot oil in batches for about 2–3 minutes. Drain on kitchen roll.

7 Cut the lemons into wedges. Wash and dry the parsley, then pick off the leaves.

8 Arrange the crispy fish on a plate and serve garnished with lemon wedges and parsley.

9 Provide a selection of soy sauce, hoisin sauce, wasabi, and sambal oelek as dips.

SERVES 4

500 g sea fish fillet

1 tsp salt

1 tsp coarsely ground pepper

2 tbsps sesame oil

2–3 tbsps rice wine

½ bunch spring onions

1 piece of fresh ginger (2–3 cm)

3 tbsps flour

2–3 eggs

100 g light sesame seeds

Groundnut oil for deep-frying

2 lemons

½ bunch parsley

Soy sauce

Hoisin sauce

Wasabi

Sambal oelek

PREPARATION TIME:
approx. 35 minutes
(plus marinating time)
398 kcal/1674 kJ

SOLE WITH KAFFIR LIME

SERVES 4

600 g sole fillets
400 g carrots
2 unwaxed kaffir limes
1 tbsp oyster sauce
2 tbsps fish sauce
4 tbsps vegetable oil
3 tbsps soy sauce
1 bunch Thai basil

PREPARATION TIME:
approx. 15 minutes
(plus marinating time)
285 kcal/1195 kJ

1 Wash the sole, dry it well, and cut it into 3 cm strips.

2 Wash, trim and peel the carrots, halve them lengthways and then into thin slices on the diagonal. Thinly slice the kaffir limes.

3 Marinate the sole for 30 minutes in the oyster and fish sauces.

4 Heat the oil in the wok and slowly cook the carrots in it. Add the kaffir lime slices and fish; mix together, and fry for about 2 minutes.

5 Deglaze with soy sauce and mix in some torn Thai basil leaves.

TIP

Sole is a very delicate fish – but unfortunately it's quite expensive as well. A cheaper alternative would be fresh cod or sea bass.

SWEET-SOUR SEA BREAM

1 Wash and pat dry the fish fillets, then remove any bones. Cut into 3 cm pieces.

2 Wash and peel the carrots, then cut them into strips with a potato peeler. Cut the leeks into 15 cm lengths, wash and shake them dry.

3 Sauté the fish pieces in 2 tbsps hot oil in the wok, only on the skin side, and take them out of the pan.

4 Sauté the vegetables in the remaining oil until they soften. Season with ketchup and sweet-and-sour sauce, then deglaze with fish sauce.

5 Put the fish back in the wok and mix it through carefully. Stir in the finely chopped coriander and serve.

SERVES 4

4 sea bream fillets, skin on (120 g each)

6 medium-size carrots

4 leeks

4 tbsps vegetable oil

2 tbsps tomato ketchup

4 tbsps sweet-and-sour sauce

2 tbsps fish sauce

2 sprigs coriander

PREPARATION TIME:
approx. 25 minutes
347 kcal/1455 kJ

SCORPION FISH WITH GINGER

1 Wash and pat dry the fish fillets, then cut them into 2 cm strips. Cut the chillies into rounds. Marinate the fish and chillies in the fish sauce for about 1 hour.

2 Cut the lemon grass into 5 cm lengths. Cut the leek on the round.

3 Wash the broccoli and break it into florets. Peel the stalk and cut it into pieces.

4 Heat half of the groundnut oil in the wok and gently fry the broccoli florets and pieces along with the lemon grass. Add the leek rings and deglaze with oyster sauce. Then mix in the grated ginger. Remove the vegetables from the wok and keep warm.

5 Heat the remaining groundnut oil in the wok and add the fish pieces. Brown carefully all over on a medium heat for about 5 minutes.

6 Arrange the broccoli and leek mixture on a dish and serve with the fish pieces.

SERVES 4

4 scorpion fish fillets, skin on (or red snapper, halibut)
2 green chillies
2 tbsps fish sauce
4 stems of lemon grass
1 leek
500 g broccoli
4 tbsps groundnut oil
4 tbsps oyster sauce
1 tbsp grated ginger

PREPARATION TIME:
approx. 20 minutes
(plus marinating time)
388 kcal/1634 kJ

STEAMED BASS

SERVES 4

250 g lotus root
250 g cucumber
250 g carrots
100 ml apple vinegar
250 ml vegetable stock
(cube)
2–3 tsps sugar
½ tsp salt
8 bamboo leaves
500 g sea bass fillets
2–3 tbsps sesame oil
2–3 tbsps ginger juice
2–3 tbsps rice wine
250 g mussels (jar)

PREPARATION TIME:
approx. 40 minutes
406 kcal/1706 kJ

1 Peel the lotus root and cut between the hollow sections. Then slice into thin rings. Peel and finely slice the cucumber and carrots.

2 Mix the apple vinegar with the vegetable stock, sugar and salt. Bring the mixture to the boil in the wok.

3 Put the prepared vegetables in the wok and simmer gently for about 5–6 minutes. Scoop them out and drain well.

4 Rinse the bamboo leaves with warm water and dry them.

5 Put the bamboo leaves in a steamer, overlapping them enough to wrap around the food you are about to cook.

6 Wash and dry the bass fillets. Mix the oil with the ginger juice and rice wine, and marinate the fish fillets for 4–5 minutes. Drain the mussels well in a sieve.

7 Spoon the vegetable mixture evenly onto the bamboo leaves. Lay the fish in its marinade on top and then the mussels. Fold the bamboo leaves over the ingredients and leave the parcel into the steamer.

8 Bring the vegetable stock to the boil again and place the steamer on a rack in the wok. Steam gently for about 10 minutes.

9 Carefully lift the vegetables and fish off the bamboo leaves and arrange on a dish to serve.

FANCY FISH BALLS

1 Wash, trim, dry and chop the spring onions. Peel the garlic cloves. Halve the chillies, de-seed them, and wash under cold running water.

2 Wash and pat dry the fish fillets, then cut them into pieces.

3 Finely mince the fish, spring onions, garlic cloves and chillies. Season the fish filling with the spices and form it into small balls.

4 Heat the oil in the wok and fry the fish balls in batches for about 5–6 minutes. Take them out of the wok and keep warm.

5 Stir the coconut milk and cream into the remaining oil in the wok along with the chilli sauce. Add the fish balls and cook on a low heat for about 10 minutes. Serve the fish balls with the sauce.

SERVES 4

1 bunch spring onions

3–4 garlic cloves

3–4 chillies

800 g sea fish fillets

Salt

Pepper

1 tbsp dried grated lemon grass

1 tbsp ground ginger

1 tsp turmeric

4–5 tbsps groundnut oil

350 ml unsweetened coconut milk

1 tbsp coconut cream

1 tbsp chilli sauce (ready-made)

PREPARATION TIME:
approx. 30 minutes
855 kcal/3592 kJ

HALIBUT WITH BEAN SPROUTS

SERVES 4

800 g halibut
Lemon juice for drizzling
Salt
Pepper
5–6 tbsps sesame oil
200 g kidney beans (tinned)
500 g bean sprouts
2–3 tbsps soy sauce
2–3 nori leaves
Lemon wedges for garnish

PREPARATION TIME:
approx. 25 minutes
482 kcal/2024 kJ

1 Wash, trim and dry the halibut, then cut it into strips. Drizzle the strips with lemon juice and season with salt and pepper.

2 Heat the oil in the wok and fry the fish strips in batches for about 4 minutes.

3 Drain the kidney beans well in a sieve. Rinse the sprouts in cold water and drain well.

4 Add the bean sprouts and kidney beans to the fish strips and stir-fry for about 3–4 minutes. Season with the soy sauce.

5 Dry-roast the nori leaves on one side in a pan and then crush them.

6 Arrange the halibut in a dish with the crushed nori leaves and serve garnished with lemon wedges.

SEAFOOD

Asian recipes using seafood are among the best in the world. They are easy to follow and make for exotic eating without great expense. Discover the culinary diversity of mussels, prawns, crab, and squid, which can be even tastier in a spicy marinade or crispy batter.

PRAWNS IN A SPICY SAUCE

1 Wash and peel the prawns, but leave the tails on. Remove the veins, pat the prawns dry, and rub with salt. Leave to soak for 10 minutes.

2 Peel the garlic and ginger and chop them very finely. Mix the ginger with the soy sauce, rice wine, sugar and pepper. Mix the cornflour to a smooth paste with a little water. Wash and trim the spring onions, then cut them finely on the diagonal.

3 Rub round the wok with a little oil, then add and heat up the rest of the oil. Sweat the garlic in it with a pinch of salt. Add the prawns and fry until they are pink, turning occasionally.

4 Add the ginger and soy sauce, kecap and fish stock, and simmer for 3 minutes. Add the cornflour and bring to the boil, stirring all the time, until the liquid starts to thicken. Serve the prawns garnished with spring onions.

SERVES 4

800 g large unpeeled raw prawns, tail on

Salt

2 garlic cloves

1 piece of fresh ginger (1 cm)

3 tbsps soy sauce

1 tbsp rice wine

2 tsps sugar

Pepper

1 tsp cornflour

4 spring onions

4 tbsps corn oil

2 tbsps kecap manis

50 ml fish stock

PREPARATION TIME:
approx. 45 minutes
(plus cooking time)
approx. 278 kcal/1166 kJ

CRAB CURRY

SERVES 4

4 brown crabs
(each weighing 250 g)
3 shallots
4 garlic cloves
2 red peppers
6 tbsps sunflower oil
1 ½ tbsps curry powder
½ bunch spring onions
2 tbsps fish sauce
(ready-made)
1 tbsp soy sauce
2 tbsps rice wine vinegar
1 tbsp lime juice
1 kaffir lime
2 tbsps palm sugar
Coriander leaves for garnish

PREPARATION TIME:
approx. 30 minutes
451 kcal/1895 kJ

1 Wash the crabs under running water and remove the claws from the body. Twist off the heads.

2 Peel and chop the shallots. Peel and finely slice the garlic. Wash the peppers, cut them in half lengthways, de-seed them, and cut into strips.

3 Heat the sunflower oil in a wok and sauté the shallots, garlic and peppers. Add the crab pieces and sprinkle on the curry powder.

4 Wash, trim and finely chop the spring onions, then add them to the wok. Cook for about 2 minutes, then pour in the fish and soy sauces, rice wine vinegar and lime juice.

5 Peel the kaffir lime, finely chop the peel and add to the wok with the palm sugar. Cook for about 6 minutes, then spoon into small bowls and serve garnished with coriander.

DID YOU KNOW?

Brown crabs live in the North Sea, Atlantic and Mediterranean and their claws are regarded as a delicacy. If you can't find brown crabs, you can also use prawns to make this dish.

KING PRAWNS WITH GARLIC

1 Wash and dry the king prawns, then deep-fry them in hot sesame oil for about 40–50 seconds until they are nice and red. Remove from the wok and drain on kitchen roll.

2 Peel and finely chop the garlic cloves. Halve the chillies, de-seed and wash them under cold running water. Slice them finely.

3 Wash and trim the spring onions, cut them on the round, and mix with the chopped chillies and garlic. Season with lemon pepper.

4 Finely chop the ginger and add to the onion and garlic mixture.

5 Heat the groundnut oil in the wok and stir-fry the vegetables for about 3–4 minutes.

6 Add the king prawns and mix together for 1–2 minutes. Serve garnished with lime wedges.

SERVES 4

900–1000 g raw king prawns, tail on and in shell

Sesame oil for deep-frying

10 garlic cloves

3–4 red chillies

1 bunch spring onions

Lemon pepper

100 g sweet-sour pickled ginger

2 tbsps groundnut oil

Lime wedges

PREPARATION TIME:
approx. 35 minutes
499 kcal/2097 kJ

MAHARAJA PRAWNS

SERVES 4

800 g cooked peeled prawns

9 garlic cloves

1 piece of freshly grated ginger (approx. 7 cm)

4 tsps tamarind paste

½ tsp turmeric

½ tsp sugar

Salt

Chilli powder

2 fresh green chillies

Vegetable oil

375 ml coconut milk

PREPARATION TIME:
approx. 20 minutes
(plus marinating time)
250 kcal/1050 kJ

1 De-vein the prawns, wash them and pat dry. Squeeze in 4 of the peeled garlic cloves. Mix with the ginger, tamarind, turmeric, sugar, 1 tsp salt and a little chilli powder. Leave to marinate for 10 minutes.

2 Trim, halve, wash, de-seed and finely chop the chillies.

3 Stir-fry 5 peeled and crushed garlic cloves in a little oil until golden. Add the prawn mixture and stir-fry for 1 minute.

4 Add the coconut milk and chillies to the wok. Bring it to the boil, season with salt and serve hot with rice.

MUSSELS WITH LEMON GRASS

1 Brush the mussels clean, removing the beards. Discard any mussels that are open.

2 Boil the mussels in water for 10 minutes, drain and remove from shells. Discard any mussels which have not opened up.

3 Peel and chop the onion and garlic. Chop the lemon grass. Halve, de-seed, wash and finely chop the chillies.

4 Heat the oil in a wok. Add the onion, garlic, lemon grass and chilli. Stir-fry for about 5 minutes on a medium heat.

5 Add the wine and fish sauce, and boil for 3 minutes. Add the mussels, stir well, cover, and simmer for a further 3–5 minutes.

6 Sprinkle with Thai basil and then serve with steamed rice.

SERVES 4

1 kg small mussels
1 onion
4 garlic cloves
2 stems lemon grass
1–2 red chillies
1 tbsp oil
250 ml white wine
1 tbsp fish sauce
16 Thai basil leaves

PREPARATION TIME:
approx. 40 minutes
(plus cooking time)
199 kcal/836 kJ

SEAFOOD STIR-FRY

SERVES 4

800 g seafood mix (frozen)
1–2 tbsps five-spice powder
1 sprig rosemary
½ bunch thyme
1 tbsp lemon juice
1 tbsp capers
20 g black olives, de-stoned
200 g sundried tomatoes in oil
4–5 tbsps groundnut oil
2–4 cl grappa
Chopped spring onion for garnish

PREPARATION TIME:
approx. 25 minutes
409 kcal/1720 kJ

1 Defrost the seafood according to the instructions on the packet. Sprinkle with five-spice powder and leave it to stand for about 5 minutes.

2 Wash and dry the herbs, then pick off and finely chop the leaves. Mix the herbs with the lemon juice and well-drained capers. Finely chop the olives and add to the mixture.

3 Drain the tomatoes well in a sieve. Then roughly chop them and add to the herb mix as well.

4 Heat the oil in the wok and stir-fry the seafood for 3–4 minutes. Scoop it out and keep warm.

5 Fry the herb, olive and tomato mixture in the remaining frying oil for 3–4 minutes. Return the seafood to the wok and heat up for 1 minute. Add a splash of grappa, arrange in a dish and, if you like, sprinkle with some spring onions before serving.

TIP

You can also make this highly aromatic dish with a firm fish. Goes well with rice and steamed vegetables.

KING PRAWNS WITH RICE WINE

1 Rinse the king prawns thoroughly under running water, dry them well, and marinate in rice wine for 30 minutes.

2 Heat the oil in the wok and melt the grated palm sugar in it. Stir in the oyster sauce, add the chilli flakes, then sear the king prawns in the mixture, stirring constantly.

3 Pour in the marinade, cover the wok with a lid, and cook the king prawns for about 3–5 minutes.

4 Scoop the king prawns out of the wok and serve drizzled with the sauce.

SERVES 4

20 large whole king prawns in shells

200 ml rice wine

6 tbsps vegetable oil

1 tsp palm sugar

4 tbsps oyster sauce

1 tsp chilli flakes

PREPARATION TIME:

approx. 15 minutes
(plus marinating time)
305 kcal/1276 kJ

223

FRIED SCALLOPS

1 Wash the scallops thoroughly, dry well and marinate in the lemon zest and sesame oil for 10 minutes.

2 Wash and trim the spring onions, then cut them into 4 cm lengths on the diagonal. De-skin the tomatoes, cut them into quarters, remove the seeds, and cut them into wedges.

3 Finely chop the peeled garlic clove and de-seeded chilli.

4 Fry the spring onions in the wok in half of the oil, add the tomatoes, ginger, garlic and chilli and fry for another 3 minutes. Season well with oyster and fish sauces. Remove from the wok.

5 Heat the rest of the oil in the wok, and fry the scallops until golden. Arrange on plates with the spring onion mixture and serve.

SERVES 4

12 prepared scallops, roe removed
1 pinch grated lemon zest
1 tbsp toasted sesame oil
1 bunch spring onions
200 g tomatoes
1 garlic clove
1 red chilli
4 tbsps sunflower oil
1 tsp freshly grated ginger
2 tbsps oyster sauce
2 tbsps fish sauce

PREPARATION TIME:
approx. 35 minutes
(plus marinating time)
142 kcal/593 kJ

DEEP-FRIED PRAWN BALLS

SERVES 4

250 g raw prawns
40 g dried rice vermicelli
1 egg
1 tbsp fish sauce
(ready-made)
100 g wheat flour
3 spring onions
1 red chilli
½ tsp bagoong (Filipino
shrimp paste)
Oil for deep-frying

PREPARATION TIME:
approx. 20 minutes
(plus cooking time)
186 kcal/780 kJ

1 Peel the prawns and remove the veins, then wash and drain them. Blend half of them into a paste in a food processor. Finely chop the rest, and mix well with the prawn paste.

2 Put the vermicelli in a bowl, cover with hot water, and leave to soak for 1 minute. Drain off the water and cut the vermicelli into short lengths.

3 Beat the egg with 150 ml water and the fish sauce. Put the flour in a bowl, make a well in the middle, and gradually add the egg mixture. Stir until the mixture is silky smooth.

4 Wash, trim and finely chop the spring onions. Wash the chilli, cut it in half and remove the stem and seeds. Chop it finely.

5 Add the prawn mixture, bagoong paste, spring onions, chilli and vermicelli and mix well.

6 Heat the oil to a high temperature. Put tablespoons of the prawn mixture into the pan and deep-fry for 3 minutes until the balls are crispy and golden. Lift them out with a slotted spoon and drain on kitchen roll.

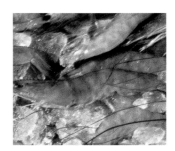

TIGER PRAWNS

1 Heat the lobster stock and soak the beans for about 30 minutes. Wash and dry the prawns.

2 Mix the oyster and fish sauces and stir in the crumbled anchovies. Also stir in the soy and chilli sauces. Marinate the prawns in the mixture for about 30 minutes.

3 Wash, trim and chop the mushrooms. Wash the chillies, halve them lengthways, remove the seeds, and chop finely. Wash and trim the runner beans, then chop them into small pieces. Wash, trim and slice the bitter melon.

4 Heat the sesame oil and sweat the vegetables in it. Stir in the curry paste and coconut cream. Season with salt and pepper.

5 Heat the groundnut oil in a wok and fry the prawns for about 4 minutes. Add the sesame seeds. Arrange the prawns and vegetables on plates and serve.

SERVES 4

125 ml lobster (or fish) stock

4 tbsps fermented black beans

750 g raw tiger prawns, shell on

7 tbsps oyster sauce

2 tbsps fish sauce

2 dried anchovies

5 tbsps light soy sauce

2 tbsps chilli sauce

300 g shiitake mushrooms

2 red/yellow habanero chillies

300 g runner beans

1 bitter melon

5 tbsps sesame oil

2 tbsps red curry paste

3 tbsps coconut cream

Salt, pepper

4 tbsps groundnut oil

3 tbsps sesame seeds

PREPARATION TIME:
approx. 20 minutes
(plus marinating and soaking time)
531 kcal/2231 kJ

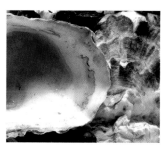

CALAMARI MEDLEY

1 Defrost the stir-fry vegetables slightly. Drain the water chestnuts, bamboo shoots and hearts of palm thoroughly in a sieve. Cut them all into thin slices.

2 Heat the oil in the wok and stir-fry all the vegetables for about 4–5 minutes. Season to taste with the spices, salt and pepper.

3 Wash and dry the squid, add it to the wok and stir-fry for a further 3–4 minutes. Wash and dry the coriander, then pick off the leaves.

4 Arrange the calamari on plates and serve sprinkled with coriander leaves.

SERVES 4

500 g Chinese stir-fry vegetables (frozen)

100 g water chestnuts (tinned)

100 g bamboo shoots (tinned)

100 g hearts of palm (tinned)

6–7 tbsps sesame oil

Ground ginger, garlic and onion powder

Salt

Pepper

500 g small squid rings

½ bunch coriander leaves

PREPARATION TIME:
approx. 30 minutes
304 kcal/1276 kJ

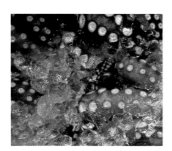  

CRISPY-COATED PRAWNS

SERVES 4

600 g prawns
4 spring onions
2 tsps salt
1 egg white
1 ½ tbsps cornflour
125 g mangetout
1 small red pepper
1 tbsp oyster sauce
1 tbsp rice wine
1 tsp sesame oil
Oil for deep-frying
½ tsp garlic
½ tsp freshly grated ginger

PREPARATION TIME:
approx. 25 minutes
(plus marinating time)
202 kcal/848 kJ

1 Peel and de-vein the prawns. Put the heads and shells in a pan and cover with water. Wash and trim the spring onions, chop them finely, and add to the pan. Bring to the boil and simmer uncovered for 15 minutes. Strain through a sieve, retaining 125 ml of the liquid, and set aside.

2 Mix 1 tsp salt through the prawns for 1 minute and rinse in cold water. Repeat the process twice, each time using ½ tsp salt. Finally, rinse thoroughly and dry the prawns.

3 Mix a whipped egg white with 1 tbsp cornflour and soak the prawns in the mixture for 30 minutes, covered.

4 Wash the mangetout. Wash the pepper, then cut it in half. Remove the stalk and seeds and cut into thin strips.

5 To make the sauce, mix together the prawn liquid with the oyster sauce, rice wine, remaining cornflour and sesame oil.

6 Heat the oil in the wok, deep-fry the prawns in batches for 1–2 minutes and lift them out with a slotted spoon. Drain on kitchen roll and keep warm.

7 Drain off all but 2 tbsps of the oil. Peel the garlic and crush it into the oil, add the ginger and stir-fry for 30 seconds. Add the mangetout and peppers and stir-fry for 2 minutes. Stir in the sauce mixture and bring to the boil. Finally, fold in the prawns and serve.

CRAYFISH WITH ARTICHOKES

1 Defrost the crayfish according to the instructions on the packet. Break off the tails and open them up, scooping out the flesh. Cut the crayfish meat into pieces.

2 Peel and finely chop the garlic cloves and shallots. Mix them in with the crayfish and season well with the spices and chilli sauce.

3 Heat the oil in the wok and stir-fry the crayfish mixture for 3–4 minutes.

4 Drain the artichoke bases well in a sieve. Chop them into small cubes and add to the wok along with the chicken stock. Gently simmer the mixture for about 1–2 minutes.

5 Mix the cornflour with a little cold water and use it to thicken the crayfish and artichoke mixture. Arrange the crayfish and artichokes on cucumber slices and serve.

SERVES 4

1–1 ½ kg crayfish
(frozen, cooked, in shell)
2 garlic cloves
4 shallots
Ground coriander, ground cumin and ground ginger
1 tbsp chilli sauce
4–5 tbsps sesame oil
300–400 g artichoke bases (tinned)
125 ml chicken stock (ready-made or cube)
1 tsp cornflour
Cucumber slices for serving

PREPARATION TIME:
approx. 30 minutes
427 kcal/1793 kJ

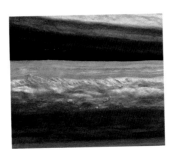 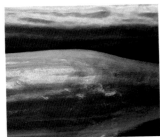 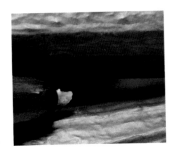

SCALLOPS WITH TOMATO

SERVES 4

1 bunch spring onions
2 garlic cloves
3 beef tomatoes
4-5 tbsps sesame oil
Salt
Pepper
Sugar
500 g prepared scallop meat
100 g mushrooms (tinned)
2 cl sherry
1 tbsp soy sauce
1 lemon

PREPARATION TIME:
approx. 20 minutes
468 kcal/1966 kJ

1 Wash, trim and dry the spring onions, then cut them finely on the round. Peel and finely chop the garlic.

2 Make cross cuts in the top of the tomatoes, dip them in boiling water for a few minutes, then plunge them in cold water and remove the skins. Dice them finely.

3 Heat the oil in the wok and stir-fry the spring onions, garlic and diced tomato for 2–3 minutes. Season with salt, pepper and a pinch of sugar.

4 Wash and pat dry the scallops, then cut them in half. Drain the mushrooms well in a sieve, then cut them in half.

5 Add the scallops and mushrooms to the vegetables, and stir-fry for 1 minute. Add the sherry and soy sauce, bring to the boil, and if necessary, season with a little more salt and pepper.

6 Arrange the scallops on a plate with lemon wedges and serve with rice.

RECIPE INDEX